A GRACIOUS CIVIC ENTERPRISE

THE STORY OF FIVE VALLEYS LAND TRUST
and the
COMMUNITY THAT MADE IT POSSIBLE

1972-2022

GREG TOLLEFSON
AND LENA VIALL

Foreword by Mae Nan Ellingson

Proceeds from the sale of this book support the work of Five Valleys Land Trust

Book design: Eileen Chontos. History, architecture, art and her natural surroundings inspire Eileen's design approach. She is a Montana native with over 40 years in the design business.

Cover image: Mary Beth Percival, "Living on the Edge," 1993, Watercolor, 23 x 17.25 in., Missoula, Montana, Monte Dolack Fine Art, www.dolack.com. Image reproduced from a watercolor painting which portrays a family of elk looking over an area of the Rattlesnake Valley, near Missoula, Montana.

Back cover: Kristi DuBois, "Clark Fork River and Missoula Valley in Autumn" 2003, Photograph, Missoula, Montana. Photo shows the Clark Fork River riparian area near Deep Creek, west of Missoula, Montana.

LCCN 2024951655

ISBN Number: 978-0-87842-721-5

PRINTED IN THE USA

Mountain Press
PUBLISHING COMPANY
P.O. Box 2399 • Missoula, MT 59806 • 406-728-1900
800-234-5308 • info@mtnpress.com
www.mountain-press.com

Land Acknowledgment

Five Valleys Land Trust acknowledges that we are in the homelands of the Séliš (Salish) and Q̓lispé (Kalispel) people. Today, we offer our respect for their history and culture, for their ancient and continuing presence in this landscape, and for the path they have shown us in caring for this place for the generations to come.

Acknowledgments

THIS BOOK, MUCH LIKE THE WORK OF PRIVATE LAND CONSERVATION, is the product of many dedicated and passionate people working together. We were honored to have the distinguished Mae Nan Ellingson write the foreword. The editing prowess of Sherry Devlin and the storytelling expertise of Peter Stark improved this story immensely. Graphic design and layout were done by the talented Eileen Chontos. Minie Smith lent us her experience to meticulously develop the index. Chelsea Feeney created our wonderful maps, and dozens of artists, photographers, and institutions helped bring the story to life. John Rimel at Mountain Press Publishing provided great professionalism and guidance. Behind it all, the support of the Five Valleys Land Trust board, staff, and community, and the hundreds of private landowners who have helped conserve western Montana's natural legacy, made this book possible.

–Greg Tollefson and Lena Viall, November 2024

CONTENTS

FOREWORD

by Mae Nan Ellingson

I HAVE NEVER WRITTEN A FOREWORD OR EVEN UNDERSTOOD THE PURPOSE OF ONE. Nevertheless, I was honored to be asked to write one for my friends Greg Tollefson and Lena Viall's book about the Five Valleys Land Trust (Five Valleys). And now that I know the ideal foreword writer is one who knows well both the author and the subject matter of the book; I believe I am definitely qualified for this task.

Greg Tollefson, who I consider to be one of the state's preeminent conservationists and an equally accomplished conservation writer, and Lena Viall, also a writer and conservationist, have written a fifty-year history of conservation in and around Missoula. It is a story of visionaries from the city and the University of Montana (UM) and the organizations they formed and nurtured and the subsequent accomplishments of those organizations through dedicated staff, committed board members, volunteers, Missoula city and county officials, donors, and private landowners.

This story begins on the cusp of Montana voters overwhelmingly deciding to hold a Constitutional Convention to rewrite their 1889 Constitution, which was written by the monied and powerful men of the timber, mining, agricultural, and banking interests. And it ends with the fiftieth anniversary of Five Valleys and coincidentally the fiftieth anniversary of the new Constitution, which was adopted on June 6, 1972, the same day Five Valleys received its 501(c)(3) determination letter from the IRS.

First, my connection to Five Valleys. In 1994, Greg invited me to attend the first Five Valleys banquet and auction at the Elks Club. Even in his telling, it was not a grand event–a taco buffet as I recall–but it was spirited and fun, and there was heartfelt and generous support for the ever-growing conservation work of the organization. Auction donors were generous, as were the bidders, and by the end of the event, I knew I had found a cause I cared about. And in Greg, I found a man whose judgment and integrity I trusted and respected. In the twenty-nine years since, I have been involved with that annual banquet in several different capacities–witnessing its phenomenal growth and success and the growing support within the business community for open space.

During that time, I also served on the board of the organization and got to witness Greg's conservation passion and indefatigable efforts on behalf of wildlife, open space, and riparian areas. Even though there have been other excellent directors of Five Valleys, it is Greg who to me epitomizes the organization's purpose and success. Given his long and deep involvement with the organization and his writing skills honed penning countless entertaining stories for the *Missoulian*, he is clearly the one to tell the story of Five Valleys.

Second, my familiarity and work with some of the founders of the predecessor organization and my work on environmental issues, including open space, predates that invitation from Greg by twenty-three years.

In the fall of 1971, John H. Toole and I were among eight Missoula County residents elected as delegates to the Constitutional Convention. During his campaign and after the election, John was engaged in talks with fellow citizens about forming an organization that would acquire park land adjacent to our rivers. Greg and Lena note an important organizational meeting in Missoula on the evening of January 20, 1972. After being in convention session in Helena all day, John drove home to attend that meeting, and there the Five Valleys River Park Association was formed. In his position as first Vice President of the Constitutional Convention, he was a supporter of the natural resource protection article in the new Constitution. John was appointed Mayor of Missoula in 1983 upon the death of Mayor Bill Cregg.

Like John Toole, I supported a strong natural resources article in the Constitution, including the right to a clean and healthful environment. After the Convention and a year of teaching high school, I attended the UM Law School and, in 1977, became deputy city attorney for the City of Missoula. In that capacity, I worked with the City Council in issuing the first open space bond in the state, which was used to acquire important land along the river and Mount Sentinel. My subsequent work as a bond lawyer with the law firm of Dorsey & Whitney, where I later met Lena, enabled me to work with both the City and County of Missoula as well as other cities and counties in the establishment of open space policies and the issuance of open space bonds. Five Valleys was often at the table in identifying projects to be funded from those bonds. As Greg and Lena note, when the open space legislation was amended to allow bond proceeds to be used for conservation easements as well as fee interests in land, a beneficial tool was created for the conservation of more precious land and resources.

The founding of Five Valleys simultaneous with the enshrinement in the Montana Constitution of a clean and healthful environment reflects an appreciation by Missoulians and Montanans for, "the quiet beauty of our state, the grandeur of our mountains and the vastness of our rolling plains."

And through the work of Five Valleys, and the passionate individuals named hereafter, these and other open spaces are still being preserved, "for this and future generations."

Mae Nan Ellingson
July 16, 2023
Missoula, Montana

Wildflowers bloom on Mount Jumbo. *–Photo by Big Sky Photography.*

PROLOGUE

"YOU DON'T KNOW WHAT YOU'VE GOT TILL IT'S GONE."

That line from Joni Mitchell's 1970 hit, *Big Yellow Taxi*, was in the air when a group of Missoulians gathered one evening in the winter of 1972, hoping to establish a system of parks and connecting trails along stream corridors in the Missoula Valley. Contrary to the line from the song, the Missoula residents who gathered that night knew full well the beauty and abundance of the natural world surrounding their valley and they were determined not to let it slip away.

A certain serendipity was in play that evening, reflecting the common wisdom that, for good things to occur, having the right people in the right place at the right time is generally a prerequisite.

That's exactly what happened fifty years ago in response to a small announcement in the *Missoulian* newspaper in January 1972:

> *A public meeting designed to gather suggestions for development of the Five Valleys River Park System will be at 7 p.m. Thursday. The meeting will be in the Ventur Center, formerly the Geology building, on the University of Montana campus.*

The idea had been percolating through the community for months, or for some, even years.

Now it was time to take action and chase a dream they all shared.

"Mount Jumbo Magic." *–Photo by Brian Christianson.*

ONE

THE VALLEYS AND THE PEOPLE

WHEN THINGS STARTED HAPPENING WITH MOUNT JUMBO, they happened quickly.

The City of Missoula, Montana, was growing. Continuing the arc that began with the first European settlements in the valley, the Missoula of the late twentieth century now saw its subdivisions begin to creep up the base of the grassy mountain slopes that ring the scenic Missoula Valley. Bulldozers traversed the hills excavating roads. Below, the city hummed.

The progress came with a price. Missoula residents had watched other cherished pieces of the natural world disappear or grow toxic with heavy metals in the valley's river waters and thick layers of smoke clogging the valley's air.

Yet, a new consciousness was in the air in Missoula, and across the nation, that great swathes of the natural world were being engulfed by human development, faster and faster.

In the preceding decades, grassroots conservation groups coalesced to help combat the rapid change. But by the early 1990s, a tipping point had come. One natural feature–literally and figuratively–loomed above them all: Mount Jumbo.

From its perch, Mount Jumbo had watched peoples come and go and make a living along the banks of the Clark Fork River for millennia. Now, it was held by private landowners, and housing developments crept up the mountain's northern flanks. But the summit and meadowy southern bulk of it still glowed golden in late afternoon sun, wildflowers burst from its slopes in spring, and on snowy winter days herds of elk emerged from its forest groves and pawed the snow away to graze on the high, open slopes for all the town to see.

Everyone knew, however, that it was just a matter of time before the private landowners sold to developers and houses wreathed the mountain from its base to its dome-like summit. Someone mentioned placing a restaurant on top. Mount Jumbo felt doomed.

In the spring of 1995, Mount Jumbo's largest private landowner died. His heirs stepped forward and approached the still-young Five Valleys Land Trust, a homegrown land conservation organization, with an offer to sell 1,000 acres encompassing a large portion of Jumbo's open flanks for fair market value–$2.75 million.

At this early point in its life, Five Valleys had never attempted anything nearly so monumental. There were severe reservations among its members and board to take on what looked like a nearly impossible task of raising close to $3 million. For a small community land trust with just two staffers, this constituted an enormous, almost unimaginable sum. It was also an enormous, almost unimaginable opportunity to change the course of the Missoula Valley's growth and its residents' connection to the landscape.

One beautiful day in the spring of 1995, Board President Chuck Tribe and Executive Director Greg Tollefson hiked to the top of the mountain's northern knob. They sat among the sprays of wildflowers and grassy slopes cascading down to the gridwork of houses on the valley floor. Retrieving sandwiches from their packs, they ate lunch and drank in the view.

From that vantage point, to Tribe at least, the solution was obvious. Tribe turned to Tollefson.

"We don't have a choice here," Tribe said. "We have to do this."

IT WAS ALWAYS ABOUT THE PLACE.

The river valleys of western Montana are magical. The Missoula Valley, spreading out beneath the towering slopes of Mount Jumbo, Mount Sentinel, and Mount Dean Stone, attests to such a glowing description. Mountain ranges encircle the valley: the Sapphires, Bitterroots, Garnets, Rattlesnake, Ninemile Divide, and Reservation Divide, all standing over the centuries as silent observers of the pageantry of life born of the ages.

Gushing from Hellgate Canyon, the Clark Fork River wends its way to a confluence with the Bitterroot River in the shadow of Blue Mountain, then barges another hundred miles downstream, carving a route through the Alberton Gorge on its way to combine forces with the glacier-fed Flathead River, making it Montana's largest moving body of water as it flows out of the state and on toward the mighty Columbia.

For millennia, the timbered slopes, grassy plains, sparkling rivers, and snow-capped peaks surrounding the valley perfectly met the needs of and sustained the Native Peoples who dwelt here or passed through, coming and going to the buffalo country east of the Continental Divide. The Séliš (Salish) and Qlispé (Kalispel) peoples, who called this broad swath of country home for generations upon generations, gathered bitterroots, camas, and huckleberries, hunted the deer and elk, trapped beaver, and fished for bull trout, westslope cutthroat trout, and Rocky Mountain whitefish that teemed in the rivers and streams, living according to the rhythms and dictates of nature. All of western Montana, from the crest of the Continental Divide to what is today the Montana-Idaho border, comprised the homeland of the Salish and Kalispel peoples.

Tepees in the Missoula Valley circa 1890, Mount Jumbo and Hellgate Canyon in the background. *–Archives & Special Collections, Mansfield Library University of Montana.*

It was here in the Missoula Valley that bitterroots, long a dietary staple for the Native Peoples, were first recorded for western science by Meriwether Lewis of the Lewis and Clark Expedition. Arriving in 1805 on their way to the Pacific, the members of that "Corps of Discovery" were the first-known non-Native visitors to the valleys. On their return east they stopped again in the summer of 1806. Here, the Corps of Discovery encountered the Salish, traded with them, and learned the favored routes to the Pacific, as well as the best trails back across the Continental Divide. A few years later, in late February 1812, British explorer David Thompson of Canada's Hudson Bay Company arrived in the valley while mapping the Columbia River from its source to the Pacific Ocean. Thompson recorded the first written reference to Mount Jumbo, describing in his journals how he climbed a "high Knowl" to sketch a map of the valley below.

Following Thompson, early French-Canadian fur trappers gave the narrow canyon where the Clark Fork River spills past Mount Jumbo into the broad Missoula Valley the name "Porte d'enfer," or "Hell's gate" in English. That rocky defile was infamous as a place where passersby were unpleasantly waylaid by Blackfeet warriors who were known to intrude on the Salish and Kalispel homelands.

Those early visits were followed by nearly a half century of occasional visitors, mostly trappers and traders, prospectors panning the mountain streams for gold, and then a few white settlers who arrived to farm the valley floors. In the 1860s, the first permanent community, a rude trading post and outbuildings, was established a few miles west of present-day Missoula. Its founders called the place Hellgate.

By 1864, the newcomers' focus and activity shifted to the eastern part of the valley, and the town, first called Missoula Mills, began to take shape. The US Army founded Fort Missoula near the confluence of the Clark Fork and Bitterroot Rivers in 1877, and census figures suggest there was a population of 2,500 in all of Missoula County by 1880. Over these early years, as settlers flooded into the fertile valleys, the Salish were forced to abandon most of their traditional homelands to this new and growing community and were relegated by US government machinations–and broken treaties–first to the Bitterroot Valley and later to a much smaller reservation located in the Jocko, Mission, and Flathead Valleys to the north.

By 1889, the year of Montana's statehood, the growing town and the surrounding valleys were bursting with optimism and enterprise. Missoula's earliest newspapers waxed poetic, exemplified by the short-lived *Missoula Weekly Gazette* in March of 1892:

> *There's a valley here–a wondrous valley–one of the brightest memories of Missoula. Its repute long precedes the sight of it. Missoula is fanned by aromas wafting from the honeyed plains. Viewing the valley from an eminence and fancy paints it a bright, enchanted garden–a mellow-hued panorama of surprises delighting the eyes and sweetening the life of a responsive beholder.*

From the beginning, the valleys surrounding Missoula were cited by local boosters not only for the obvious scenic grandeur, but also for the potential wealth lying untapped in vast stores of timber, unexplored mineral deposits, and the rich, unplowed topsoil of the valley bottoms. It is not certain who coined the term "Five Great Valleys," but it began to appear regularly in the *Missoulian* newspaper soon after it began publication in 1891. Early accounts identified those five valleys as the Hellgate Valley, from the mouth of Hellgate Canyon east to the headwaters of the Clark Fork River–then known as the Missoula River–near Butte; the Blackfoot Valley to the northeast; the Bitterroot Valley to the south; the Frenchtown Valley to the west; and the Flathead Valley to the north.

Once it became apparent that the true center of activity would surround the new community of Missoula, references to the Frenchtown Valley were supplanted by the Missoula Valley. Early *Missoulian* editor, Arthur L. Stone, who later became the first dean of the School of Journalism at UM, used the term often in editorials and reporting. The Missoula Chamber of Commerce touted the growth and business opportunities abounding in the Five Great Valleys. Realtor W. R. Glasscock's regular ad in the *Missoulian* offering properties for sale carried the bold headline, "In The Five Great Valleys."

Progress was the dominant theme for local boosters, exemplified succinctly in a blurb on the *Missoulian* editorial page in 1912:

> *"Missoula is the center of five great valleys. The example should be for the exploitation of them all."*

And so it was.

THE FIVE GREAT VALLEYS

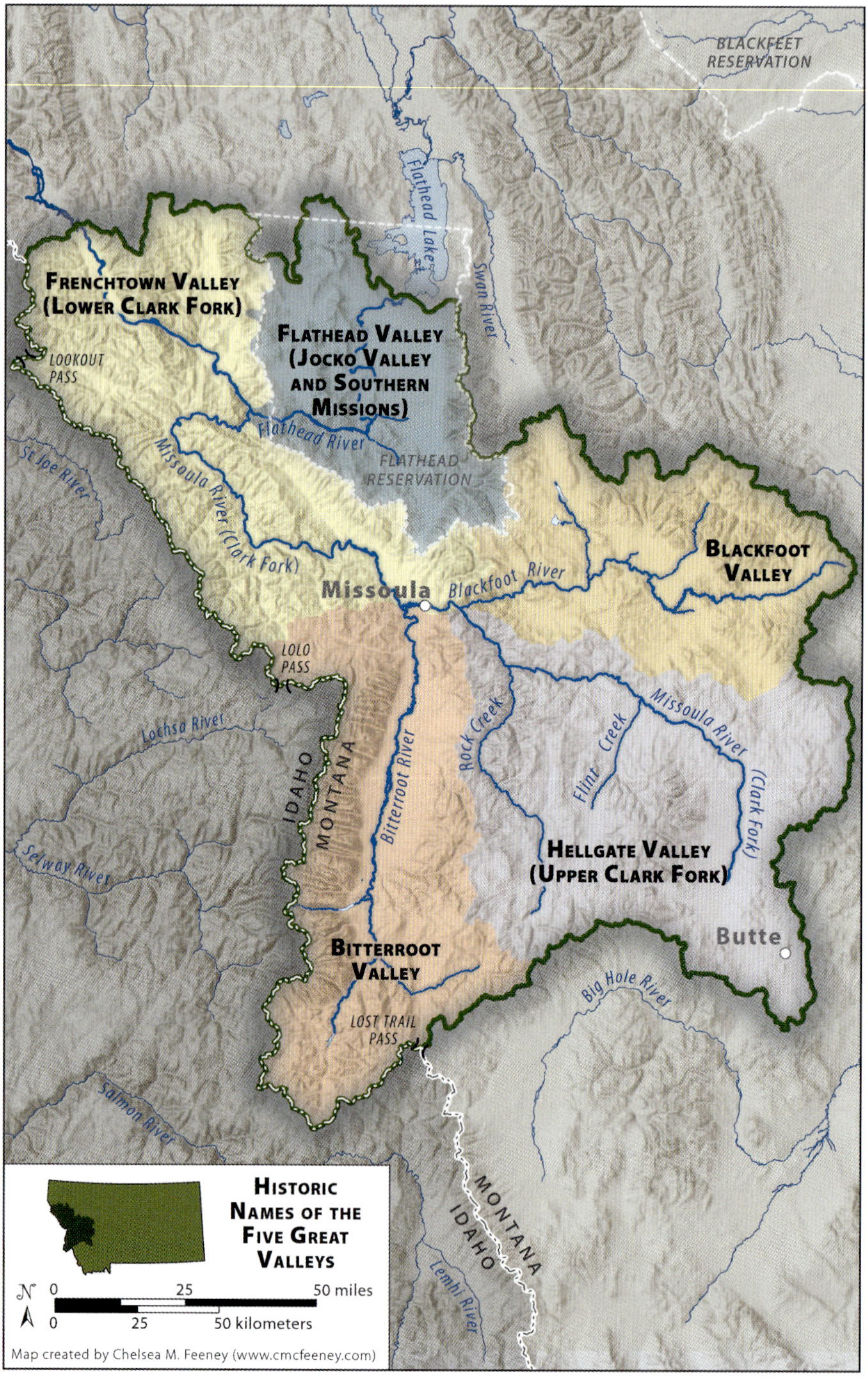

Downtown Missoula circa 1890, with Mount Jumbo in the background. *–Archives & Special Collections, Mansfield Library University of Montana.*

In 1893, the same year Missoula Mills was incorporated into the Town of Missoula, the Northern Pacific Railroad arrived, establishing its depot at the north end of Higgins Avenue near the foot of what would become Waterworks Hill. Rail service transformed the Five Great Valleys. Missoula County's population boomed nearly sixfold, to 14,000 residents, by 1900.

The Town of Missoula became a bustling center of commerce, industry, agriculture, and education. Young minds arrived via train from across the country to study at UM, founded two decades prior. A hydroelectric dam was built at Milltown in 1908, lighting up the young city. The Anaconda Copper Mining Company ran a giant lumber mill next door at Bonner, swallowing up the huge ponderosa pine logs rafted down the Blackfoot River. The electrified Milwaukee Railroad arrived in 1910, establishing its handsome depot along the bank of the Clark Fork River in the heart of town, its line running parallel to the Northern Pacific's on the opposite side of the river.

A water system tapping into the mountain lakes and streams of the Rattlesnake drainage was constructed by the nascent Montana Power Company. The US Forest Service (USFS) established headquarters for all of its Northern Region in the Federal Courthouse and Post Office building on East Broadway. Missoula County's population swelled to 23,500 by 1910.

Missoula and the rest of western Montana kept growing, faster and faster. By 1960, a century after the founding of the Hellgate outpost, Missoula had become the regional hub that its early boosters had hoped. Missoula County's 45,000 residents ensured the hum of industry was ever present. The clang of coupling and uncoupling freight cars could be heard all night long. The Five Great Valleys' vast forests continued to feed a hungry timber industry, as demonstrated by a huge pulp mill that started operation near Frenchtown in the 1950s. At night, the glow of tepee burners–huge conical steel structures that incinerated the tons of sawdust created at local lumber mills–lit the skies like giant torches.

Yet, amid the progress and apparent prosperity, all was not necessarily copacetic. More than a century of relatively unregulated exploitation of timber and mineral resources, unchecked harvesting of fish and wildlife resources, and ever-increasing residential and commercial development inflicted a visible toll on the abundance and beauty that gave life to the valley. Some citizens began to voice concerns about the pace of growth. They pointed to the increasing subdivision and development of lands along the rivers and across the hillsides, as well as the loss of agricultural lands in all directions from town. Disputes arose over timber harvest and mining practices in the nearby mountains. Scientists took note of endangered species, loss of wildlife habitat, and mining wastes contaminating the rivers and killing fish.

Panoramic of downtown Missoula circa 1920. *–Photo by R. H. McKay, Archives & Special Collections, Mansfield Library University of Montana.*

Doris Milner, a local conservationist, speaks to attendees of a G.A.S.P. rally at the Frenchtown pulp mill. *–Archives & Special Collections, Mansfield Library University of Montana.*

Air pollution became a concern. The mountain valleys spawned temperature inversions in winter and the air, choked with smoke from tepee burners and thousands of residential fireplaces and coal furnaces, as well as foul air billowing from the stacks at the pulp mill at Frenchtown, constituted a toxic stew that posed a clear threat to public health. In fact, the air pollution was so bad that, in 1968, it spawned the creation of a group of concerned citizens called Gals Against Smog and Pollution (G.A.S.P.). G.A.S.P.'s objective, according to an April 12, 1968, *Missoulian* article, was, "to affirm the belief that clean air is vital to the mental and physical well-being of the members of this community, to the maintenance of property values, and to the aesthetic appreciation of Missoula's natural surroundings."

While new homes crept higher and higher up the grassy slopes and foothills around town, lumber mills, stockyards, blacksmith shops, meatpacking plants and commercial enterprises of all kinds crowded along the Clark Fork River's banks in the valley below. The river provided the nearest place to dispose of trash, including effluent from slaughterhouses and abandoned vehicles. In fact, once automobiles came along, junked vehicles soon provided a quick and easy answer to the need for riprap material to stabilize streambanks. Rusted car bodies can still be found along some stretches of the Clark Fork and Bitterroot Rivers today.

Slowly, residents of the Missoula Valley began to take note of just what was becoming of those natural values so critical to the physical and spiritual well-being of the entire population. People were simply becoming more and more aware that many of the natural values and resources that had so long enriched the lives of all, and had been more-or-less taken for granted, were in imminent danger of being further degraded or lost entirely.

This awareness, of course, rose not as a phenomenon unique to the Missoula Valley, but as a nationwide–and worldwide–concern. During the 1960s and 1970s, the United States underwent a renaissance in understanding the importance of protecting the natural processes that sustain life and lend quality to the lives of all. Clearly, the rapid changes in the natural world brought on by human population growth, industrial and agricultural activities, and commercial and residential development threatened the ecological framework of our own existence on the planet.

A bipartisan response from federal, state, and local governments, urged on by a growing hue and cry from a burgeoning number of conservation groups, resulted in the adoption of legislation that codified this renewed awareness of our dependence on the natural world and our stewardship responsibility to protect the vital biological systems–water, air, forests, grasslands, wildlife, and, yes, natural beauty–of our nation, and more particularly for us, of the State of Montana.

Although there exists a long and celebrated legacy of conservation efforts paralleling the arc of US history, from countless generations of Native Americans who lived in relative harmony with the natural world, to famed US naturalists like Thoreau and Muir, and the establishment of national parks like Yellowstone in 1872, a renewed sense of conservation awareness grabbed the spotlight in 1964 when Congress passed the Wilderness Act. Reaching boldly toward a new concept of conservation, the Wilderness Act provided for preservation of the wildest and most-pristine places across the American landscape, places that were falling like dominoes to extractive economic forces, enshrining them with permanent protection.

"A wilderness, in contrast with those areas where man and his own works dominate the landscape," the Wilderness Act explicitly states, "is hereby recognized as an area where the earth and its community of life are untrammeled by man, where man himself is a visitor who does not remain."

Western Montana emerged as a focal point for wilderness protection, with the beloved Bob Marshall Wilderness among those first given protection under the Act. Now known affectionately as "the Bob," that swath of wild country straddling the Continental Divide a short drive from Missoula serves as evidence of the effectiveness of the proactive approach to conservation that has become foundational for much of the conservation accomplished since.

The passage of the Wilderness Act set the stage for sweeping activity in the realm of conservation. In the United States, we celebrated the first Earth Day in 1970.

The celebration grew out of an era of grassroots activism in the 1960s. It was further fueled by Rachel Carson's book, *Silent Spring*, and environmental disasters such as Ohio's Cuyahoga River catching on fire in 1969 and a major oil well blowout in the Pacific Ocean off Santa Barbara the same year. Earth Day's organizers anticipated political activists on college campuses would quickly rally behind the notion of a shared societal obligation to take better care of the natural world, but they were gratified to learn that suburban housewives and schoolteachers were some of the movement's most-impassioned followers. An estimated 20 million Americans marched or otherwise recognized the first Earth Day. Where conservation formerly had lingered on America's political fringes, it was now clearly a major movement.

What followed was a cascade of far-reaching federal legislation that underscored the need to protect the natural world for the good of all. These momentous pieces of legislation included:

- National Environmental Policy Act, 1970
- Creation of the Environmental Protection Agency, 1970
- Federal Clean Air Act, 1970
- Montana Environmental Policy Act, 1971
- Federal Clean Water Act (complete overhaul and update), 1972

This surging national spirit of conservation and environmental consciousness in the late 1960s and early 1970s found fertile ground in Montana. A year after

Earth Day was celebrated nationwide, the Montana Legislature passed a unique and consequential law, the Montana Environmental Policy Act. The following year, 1972, ushered in another landmark event, when Montanans took up drafting a new state Constitution.

Montana's original Constitution, passed in 1889, was, "a wordy, creaky document that provided for a weak state government," according to state capitol reporter Chuck Johnson, who covered the 1972 Constitutional Convention. Copper King William A. Clark had served as president of that original constitutional convention, noted Johnson, and it, "treated the copper mining companies well."

One circumstance that led to the drafting of a remarkable document at the 1972 Constitution Convention was the Montana Supreme Court ruling that no sitting politicians could serve as delegates to the Convention. With politicians barred, it became a citizen effort.

Fiercely proud of the wild beauty and natural abundance of Montana's magnificent landscape, Convention delegates sought to acknowledge their rich heritage in the preamble to the new Montana Constitution with these words:

> *We the people of Montana grateful to God for the quiet beauty of our state, the grandeur of our mountains, the vastness of our rolling plains, and desiring to improve the quality of life, equality of opportunity and to secure the blessings of liberty for this and future generations do ordain and establish this constitution.*

Just a few paragraphs later, the delegates codified a unique right into Montana's new guiding document:

> ***Article II, Declaration of Rights, Section 3. Inalienable Rights:***
> *All persons are born free and have certain inalienable rights. They include the right to a clean and healthful environment and the rights of pursuing life's basic necessities, enjoying and defending their lives and liberties, acquiring, possessing and protecting property, and seeking their safety, health and happiness in all lawful ways. In enjoying these rights, all persons recognize corresponding responsibilities.*

This right was listed before the right to freedom of religion or the right to freedom of speech. A few pages later, this clear commitment to environmental protection was further emphasized and given legal weight:

> ***Article IX. Environmental and Natural Resources, Section 1. Protection and Improvement:***
> *(1) The state and each person shall maintain and improve a clean and healthful environment in Montana for present and future generations.*
> *(2) The legislature shall provide for the administration and enforcement of this duty.*
> *(3) The legislature shall provide adequate remedies for the protection of the environmental life support system from degradation and provide adequate remedies to prevent unreasonable depletion and degradation of natural resources.*

So, it should have come as no surprise that, in and around Missoula, people saw what was happening to the land and water and decided it was time to act. And for those pioneers, it began with the rivers–the moving water that animates our lives and feeds our souls.

natural values that made the Missoula Valley and the City of Missoula such a wonderful place to live, work, and raise families.

In city and county government, and in the community at large, there was a growing sense that it was time for action. Development was haphazard, with few planning tools in use to address it.

The tipping point came in late 1971 when a rezoning proposal surfaced for a 20-acre plot of land at the mouth of Hellgate Canyon, part of a larger parcel known as Hughes Gardens. The popular vegetable farming operation had been part of the local landscape since the turn of the twentieth century. Regular ads in the *Missoulian* classifieds announced when cucumbers, sweet corn, radishes, onions, green beans, and other vegetables were ripe and ready. Generations of Missoula families relied on Hughes Gardens for fresh produce. Hundreds of Missoula teenagers found their first jobs working at the gardens, especially at harvest time. In 1971, a 20-acre parcel carved from Hughes Gardens came up for sale. The parcel had recently been annexed by the City of Missoula and had promptly been zoned for residential development. Once sold, the buyers quickly requested a zoning change to allow for commercial development.

The zoning change was necessary for developers' plans for unspecified commercial development on the site. Despite considerable public opposition, the City Council agreed to rezone the land.

Concurrently, a debate was ongoing about planned construction of a Smitty's Pancake Parlor that would span Rattlesnake Creek just north of Broadway near the Madison Street bridge over the Clark Fork River.

Two new groups emerged in the community in opposition to those plans, and in anticipation of possible future developments that might encroach upon Missoula's streambanks or that might threaten the natural beauty and values.

The Missoula Citizens Lobby, with UM math professor Robert McKelvey as its primary spokesman, protested the developments. The group suggested, in the alternative, a planning process to guide community growth that considered environmental and related social values. Another UM faculty member, geography professor Chris Field, echoed McKelvey's concerns on behalf of the Community Improvement Council. Both groups suggested that rather than allow the proposed developments, a broader, long-term view of a river park system for Missoula should be considered, with the Hughes Gardens parcel as its logical anchoring place.

The City Council refused to reconsider the zoning change for the Hughes Gardens parcel, and on July 18, 1972, investors announced their plans to move ahead with construction of a 100-unit motel on 4.7 acres of the property. Also in 1972, despite significant and loud public opposition and legal challenges, the pancake parlor was able to move ahead with construction. The grand opening was held on December 12, 1972. The dinner special was prime rib for $3.95.

The efforts of the two community groups, the Missoula Citizens Lobby and the Community Improvement Council, had succeeded in gently encouraging a new sensitivity and awareness among community leaders at a time when these very issues were becoming vital to the future of a rapidly growing city. Even as those early losing battles were being fought, the die had been cast for yet another new organization.

In early January of 1972, nearly a year before the grand opening prime rib special at Smitty's, the *Missoulian* printed a full-page feature titled "On Missoula's Riverfront." It was a package of stories by reporter Larry Pederson that detailed the history of riverfront development in Missoula and the importance of protecting floodplains. It also explored the potential benefits to the community, for business and the public at large that would derive from more sensitive planning that incorporates public access, scenic beauty, and habitat protection.

"The city has turned its back on the river," asserted Dave Crow, Missoula City-County Planner, in one of the "On Missoula's Riverfront" stories. "But now, a new attitude toward riverfront development is taking root," he continued. "It's time to turn our faces and energies toward the rivers so that our community will grow and prosper."

Another story told of the ongoing work of Bruce Bugbee, who had started as a volunteer fresh out of UM quietly toiling on plans to remake local riverfronts to enhance natural habitat and scenic values, while allowing pedestrian access. Now as project director for the Regional Planning Association, a consortium of nine Montana cities and counties west of the Continental Divide, Bugbee had been putting together a grand scheme: A trail system that would nearly encircle the community of Missoula, following river and stream corridors up the Bitterroot River to Pattee Creek, up Pattee Creek and down Deer Creek, back to the Clark Fork River five miles east of town.

A few days after the "On Missoula's Riverfront" *Missoulian* piece, Gerald Coutant, chief landscape architect for the USFS's Northern Region, gave a lecture on UM's campus. His talk offered another vision for long-term and thoughtful development of an interlocking system of parks, trails, and public spaces along river and stream corridors in Missoula. In the days that followed, Coutant repeated the presentation and accompanying slideshow for a number of groups around the community. Here is how Coutant's presentation began:

> ***Man and the River***
> *The beauty of water in all its forms is legendary. The still waters of the Psalmist, the fountains of Rome, the cataracts of Niagara, the road of the surf–through history, such waters have inspired innumerable works of art and poetry. For the utilitarian values of water, most of America's great cities have been built on rivers, lakes or ocean. For recreation and inspiration, Americans throng to the water's edge, to participate in water sports as well as to enjoy fishing and the sight of waterfowl in flight. Some of the most pressing problems in conserving resources of tremendous value to man's welfare and spirit are centered on water and where land and water meet. Too often in the past, river flows were harnessed without adequate thought for their scenic, recreational, fish and wildlife, and human values. Shorelines were denuded of forest and streams were filled with waste. Today, industrial pollutants and city sewage too often reduce water quality or make waters unusable for drinking or recreation and offensive to the eye. Waters and waterways in and near population centers serve the public best in some instances if the public has access to them. Unfortunately, there is often no such public access.*

Discussions continued around Missoula and enough interest was shown that riverfront planning advocates scheduled a public meeting for the evening of January 20, with this modest announcement tucked away on page 8 of the *Missoulian*:

> *A public meeting designed to gather suggestions for development of the Five Valleys River Park System will be at 7 p.m. Thursday. The meeting will be in the Ventur Center, formerly the Geology building, on the University of Montana campus.*

Twenty people showed up at that first meeting. They came from across the community and included UM professors Robert McKelvey, Chris Field, and George Brabb; Arnold Bolle, dean of the School of Forestry and future president of the Wilderness Society, and his wife Helen; then Missoula mayor and future lieutenant governor of Montana George Turman; future Missoula mayor and Vice President of Montana's 1972 Constitutional Convention John Toole, a local businessman; Gerald Coutant and Robert Neville, both landscape architects for the USFS; local architect Jim McDonald; Bob Knight, a young attorney, and his wife Ellen, a graduate student in aquatic biology at UM; Jean Robbins, a Missoula homemaker; UM student Dennis Williamson; and Dean Ricer, UM grounds crew foreman and horticulturist. Interestingly, Toole rushed home from his duties as vice president of the Montana Constitutional Convention to attend.

Park Proposal Discussion Set

A public meeting designed to gather suggestions for development of the Five Valleys River Park System will be at 7 p.m. Thursday. The meeting will be in the Ventur Center, formerly the Geology building, on the University of Montana campus.

The January 1972 *Missoulian* ad that launched the Five Valleys River Park Association. — Missoulian *archives.*

The meeting began with Coutant once again sharing his presentation, "Man and the River." This time, it was like preaching to the choir. Many of the attendees had already heard it. Those who hadn't already knew and agreed with the importance of such an endeavor. They were ready to roll up their sleeves and get something done. And they did.

They appointed a steering committee to guide creation of an organization that was to become the Five Valleys River Park Association (FVRPA). Sixteen of those people in attendance agreed to serve on the committee. George Brabb was named president; George Turman, vice-president; Bob Knight, secretary; and Jean Robbins, treasurer.

In May, the group finalized Articles of Incorporation, which were filed with the state on June 6, 1972. The document listed Bob Knight, John Toole, Robert Neville, Gerald Coutant, Robert McKelvey, George Truman, Chris Field, George Brabb, Jean Robbins, Dean Ricer, Jim McDonald, and Dennis Williamson as the Board of Directors. Now the fledgling organization could begin to take the necessary steps to become a qualified non-profit organization, or a 501(c)(3), according to the IRS.

Next, they began crafting a comprehensive vision statement to share with the city and county governments and the citizens of Missoula. Complicated though it would be in execution, the plan would be simple to encapsulate.

"Our goal," recounted Helen Bolle, who attended the organizational meeting with her husband, Arnold, "was to have river parks stretching from Milltown Dam to the confluence of the Clark Fork and Bitterroot rivers."

Over the weeks that followed, the group moved ahead professionally, developing a detailed planning process, including establishing goals and objectives, outlining procedures, identifying information to be gathered, identifying professionals willing to assume roles in assembling a complete survey of the resource values and characteristics of the stream corridors, and finding volunteers for assorted tasks. The wordsmiths in the group continued to hone their vision, which was unveiled in an open letter to local government and the community at large. That vision was summarized with these words:

> *The river park system contemplated will take many years to develop, perhaps becoming a continuing project capable of linking generations in gracious civic enterprise. Ideally, the system should start upstream, at least as far as East Missoula on the Clark Fork and the big bend by the weighing station on the Bitterroot. Thus, both important city entrances could be visually preserved and enhanced. The downstream system should include substantial sections of the cottonwood flats floodplain to, and including, the river junction. Branch connections to ensure continuous access will have to be developed in all of the connecting creeks, Rattlesnake, Grant, Pattee, and Miller ... Civic pride and regional identity would logically attend this as an aspect of the effort to require identification as "Garden City."*

The new Five Valleys River Park Association was up and running.

With the blessing of Mayor Turman and, by association, the City of Missoula, FVRPA opened a temporary office in the basement of City Hall. At first, this involved gaining access to a certain key that was kept at the Police Department, which only certain members of the FVRPA were entrusted with. That soon became unnecessary when Bob Knight cleared some space in his downtown law office so FVRPA work could continue there.

Much of the first two years were spent fleshing out the river parks plan, identifying properties and ownership, and gathering natural resource data, but there was also the task of building a constituency.

Bob and Ellen Knight, who attended that first meeting, described the early work of FVRPA as a time of engaging with community members so the river park system would be a true community effort. FVRPA worked to educate the public, identified and cultivated partnerships, met with government officials, and worked on creative approaches to securing key parcels of land.

"Well before it was even anything," recalled Ellen Knight, "Five Valleys had somehow attracted a number of people with skills in a variety of areas. And so, we set about raising some consciousness about the riverfront conservation, how we might go about it, and creating some maps to identify properties that we might try to protect."

The group set out to educate the public in a variety of ways. They created a speaker's bureau, sending board members and community volunteers out to speak to and engage in discussions about the benefits of planning a river park system with church groups, neighborhood groups, and service organizations. As word spread, more opportunities arose. FVRPA conducted "river walks" led by resource professionals or naturalists to introduce residents to new ways of looking at the landscape, wildlife, and vegetation in the hopes it might capture their imaginations.

An overarching concern–how to fund the grand dream–also had to be addressed. FVRPA members researched the potential sources of the money it was going to take to get things done. Once some of those sources were identified, the group waded into the politics of securing such funding.

The first fundraising success was announced on August 23, 1972. It came in the form of a $100 seed money grant from the America the Beautiful Fund. In FVRPA's early years, this source provided additional funding that proved instrumental in helping to build the organization.

Besides data collection, large-scale planning, funding, and community outreach, there were other emergent matters that demanded immediate attention. Among the activities that FVRPA members participated in were:

- Fort Missoula open space planning. As residential and commercial development began to encircle the Fort Missoula area on three sides, with the

Bitterroot River buffering the south boundary, local government and the general public engaged in discussions aimed at assuring the open character of the Fort area remained intact, and further development would focus on public recreational use.

- Floodplain zoning. Concerns about inappropriate development in floodplains spurred an effort to complete and update mapping of Clark Fork and Bitterroot floodplains and establish appropriate zoning to protect those floodplains, particularly in the area around Buckhouse Bridge and Fort Missoula, as well as the downtown area.
- Milwaukee Depot. With the Milwaukee Railroad no longer using its depot in Missoula, discussions were underway with the City of Missoula about possible purchase of the iconic railroad depot as a potential focal point for a broad riverfront trail system.
- Disposition of USFS lands along the Bitterroot River in the Blue Mountain area. A variety of proposals that would have moved certain USFS parcels into City of Missoula ownership for parks were under consideration. FVRPA advocated for permanent designation of the land for parks. The USFS eventually decided to retain title to the land in question, and it has been permanently identified and developed as park and recreation land, now known as the Maclay Flat Nature Trail.
- Early discussions related to a potential city open space bond. The research into funding opportunities suggested open space bonds might be a way to fund major real estate acquisitions by the City of Missoula. These discussions would bear fruit almost a decade later.

As would prove to be the case throughout the years ahead, there was far more to be done than FVRPA could reasonably expect to accomplish. But, as would also be the case for its successor organization, FVRPA was blessed with the willingness of an always engaged and professional board, and later staff, to tackle challenges that seemed at first unsurmountable.

The association reached a significant milestone on August 11, 1972, when the Internal Revenue Service approved its application for designation as a 501(c)(3) non-profit corporation. The directors listed on the application included: Robert Knight, John Toole, Robert Neville, Gerald Coutant, George Turman, Chris Field,

George Brabb, Jean Robbins, Audra Browman, William Cardon, Louis Nordbye, Arnold Bolle, Randolph Jacobs, and Mark Hubbell.

The new non-profit got right down to the business of identifying suitable projects and getting them done. Seeking to increase public awareness of the growing movement for protection of the river corridor, FVRPA seized on the idea of using the Missoula Chamber of Commerce-sponsored May Spectacular Hellgate River Race as a springboard into the limelight. The result was a half-page *Missoulian* article by Don Schwennesen with the bold type headline, "Area Parks People Planning A New Kind of River Race."

"We're conducting a race for the preservation of the river," FVRPA board member Bob Knight proclaimed. The article went on to detail the vision and describe the efforts of the organization, while also serving as the first public appeal for help in financing that work. The *Missoulian* article was also the public unveiling of the organization's brand-new logo. In the article, Schwennesen noted that, although FVRPA did have some projects in mind, representatives of the organization were, as yet, reluctant to identify them. However, it wasn't long before the first project was announced.

The logo of the Five Valleys River Park Association. –*Five Valleys Land Trust collections.*

The first surprisingly complex effort came along in September 1973. To celebrate the 100th Anniversary of the First National Bank, bank President Randy Jacobs, who had become a FVRPA board member, quietly engineered the bank's purchase of a key piece of river property near the heart of the Missoula: the Van Buren Street Island, located where the old Van Buren Street bridge (now a walking bridge) spanned the Clark Fork adjacent to the UM campus. First National Bank, in turn, donated the land to FVRPA. FVRPA then leveraged the island as the basis for a grant application to the Bureau of Outdoor Recreation (then an agency of the Department of Interior) to secure funds to help develop the parcel into a park.

Jacobs Island in fall color, with Mount Sentinel rising above it. *–Photo by Paul Queneau.*

That accomplished, the island was turned over to the City of Missoula. The property was renamed Jacobs Island in honor of the founding family of First National Bank, later renamed First Interstate Bank. It remains a popular local river access and dog park today.

The bank received national recognition from the Interior Department for, "Outstanding contribution from the private sector that provided additional outdoor recreation opportunities and helped establish a national legacy of parks." Spearheading the project were Missoula Mayor John Toole and attorney Bob Knight. Knight would continue to play a major role, both in his donation of thousands of hours of the finest legal work possible and in bringing a lasting vision to local and statewide conservation work for decades to come.

This project also served as a template for what became a legacy of collaboration among FVRPA, other local organizations, government agencies, and the private sector. The Jacobs Island project helped leverage a second grant from the Bureau of Outdoor Recreation, which in turn funded work on an expanding palette of possible projects.

With these successes, momentum began to build for conservation projects conducted under the auspices of FVRPA. That same year, 1973, David J. Maclay, a civic-minded Lolo area rancher who had acquired a number of properties in and around the Missoula Valley, donated a 10-acre island parcel on the Clark Fork River in the Orchard Homes area north of Hiberta Street to FVRPA. This parcel, which came to be known as Maclay Island, was held by the organization for many years until it became possible for the City of Missoula to take ownership as part of its park system.

From left: David J. Maclay, George Brabb, and John Toole tour Maclay Island in the Clark Fork River, February 1973. –*Missoulian archives.*

In 1974, FVRPA helped facilitate the purchase of 380 acres at the confluence of the Clark Fork and Bitterroot Rivers by the Montana Department of Fish, Wildlife and Parks (Montana FWP). Kelly Island, a rich and diverse riparian area, offered wonderful wildlife habitat in a classic cottonwood bottomland ecosystem, provided tremendous recreational opportunity, and helped define the wildland-urban interface. The popular river access still provides those benefits today. Longtime locals also attest that it was at Kelly Island, or thereabouts, where the Hellgate Treaty of 1855 was signed between the US Government and the Bitterroot Salish, Pend d'Oreille, and Kootenai Tribes, not at Council Grove where the treaty's monument stands today.

Also in 1974, FVRPA sponsored a successful riverbank cleanup, drawing volunteers from all across the Missoula community in support of their local river.

The following year brought a new focus to the riparian corridor along Rattlesnake Creek, in the form of two projects in particular. One of the fundamental aims of the FVRPA was, of course, creating connecting trail systems along the rivers and creeks feeding into the Missoula Valley. Rattlesnake Creek, with Greenough Park near its terminus with the Clark Fork, was the most visible and closest to the city core of those streams. A trail system stretching the length of Rattlesnake Creek, from its mouth at the Clark Fork River, through Greenough Park, and all the way to the Lolo National Forest boundary four miles to the north, was one of the highest priorities.

George Brabb (center) with members of the Five Valleys River Park Association at the 1974 Clark Fork River cleanup. –*Five Valleys Land Trust collections.*

This vision for a "greenway" got another boost from a group of Rattlesnake Valley residents who had formed the Pineview Park Association, basing their name on Pineview Park, a park located about halfway between the mouth of Rattlesnake Creek and the national forest boundary. The Association asked FVRPA for assistance in acquiring a 9-acre parcel on the creek, adjacent to Pineview Park. Seeing a key piece of the Rattlesnake trail corridor, FVRPA agreed. FVRPA submitted and secured another grant from the Bureau of Outdoor Recreation and worked to raise the matching funds necessary to purchase the land from the Green family. The family donated a portion of the land's value in honor of their late son, Tom Green, hence the name the park bears today.

Just a bit farther downstream, another parcel was preserved in collaboration with the Henry Bugbee family along with Missoula County, The Nature Conservancy, Montana FWP, and FVRPA. The Bugbee Preserve, like Tom Green Park, involved what has come to be a standard in conservation transactions, that is a "bargain sale" in which the seller donates a significant part of the fair market value as a charitable contribution to a non-profit conservation organization. The Bugbee family did just that, and the balance of the fair market value price was covered using funds secured with the help of the Montana congressional delegation from the federal Land and Water Conservation Fund. The Land and Water Conservation Fund would be a critical source of funding in many of the projects completed in the years to come.

Once again, Bob Knight played the leading role for FVRPA in getting these projects through the complicated, necessarily bureaucratic process of transferring the land into public ownership. The Nature Conservancy provided the know-how to access Land and Water Conservation Fund monies. Bruce Bugbee was instrumental in the effort and would remain a major player in conservation land transactions around Missoula and throughout the State of Montana in the decades that followed.

On the state level, 1975 became a turning point for private land conservation efforts in Montana with the passage of the Open-Space Land and Voluntary Conservation Easement Act. Since 1964, the Internal Revenue Service had been recognizing gifts that provided permanent legal protection of certain natural values, at first focusing on scenic values, as charitable contributions for tax purposes. Over time, the protection of wildlife habitat, recreational opportunities, agricultural uses, and historic values were also deemed acceptable. Those protections would come in the form of a legal encumbrance on a property title that became known as a "conservation easement." The value of such a gift would be based upon a formal appraisal of the property *before* such an easement and its encumbrances had been placed upon a property, as well as *after* the easement and its encumbrances were in place. The difference between the two figures would be considered the value of the charitable gift. Such easements would be in force in perpetuity.

While the concept itself had evolved, a formal legal framework for these transactions had not yet been incorporated into federal or Montana law. Concern over the need for more tools and planning to address environmental protection in the face of increasing population growth and unregulated urban and suburban sprawl spawned considerable, often bitter, debate in communities across the state and in the Montana Legislature. A highly respected national conservation organization, The Nature Conservancy, had come on the scene and was promoting the notion that Montana should craft its own framework for such legal instruments to provide an innovative and attractive new tool for conservation. It didn't happen overnight, but due to the collaborative efforts of a team of lawyers, legislators, landowners, and conservationists, the Montana Open-Space Land and Voluntary Conservation Easement Act was passed in 1975. FVRPA's Bob Knight was one of the attorneys credited with crafting the Montana legislation, which became a model for subsequent federal legislation and for similar legislation in other states around the country.

With passage of conservation easement legislation, what would come to be known as the land trust movement established a solid foothold in Montana. The Montana chapter of The Nature Conservancy used conservation easements as a primary tool in its work, focusing many of its early efforts in the Big Blackfoot River area. In 1978, the first Montana-based land trust, the Montana Land Reliance out of Helena, started to work with landowners, and especially ranchers and farmers, across the state to protect important elements of the precious Montana landscape.

In Missoula, FVRPA continued to do the spade-work necessary to secure community investment in the conservation future of the Missoula Valley. FVRPA also accepted several more gifts of conservation property along the Clark Fork River: a 30-acre parcel near Clinton from David Maclay, a 5-acre riverfront strip in Hellgate Canyon from attorney Jack L. Green II, and a 14-acre river island in the Big Flat area from Michael Heutmaker, a Washington State businessman.

Along with land ownership comes the responsibility for managing the land in a responsible, environmentally sensitive manner. Benign neglect might be the best way to describe FVRPA's early years of landholding. The parcels received by the organization were undeveloped, adjacent to the Clark Fork River, and largely made up of riparian habitat. There was little public use of the parcels and no active management. In the years to come, the concept of responsible land stewardship would become a fundamental element of the mission of the successor organization.

Years later, the 30 acres at Clinton would be transferred to the adjacent Clinton School District for use in school programs. The Hellgate Canyon property was donated to the City of Missoula as riverside park land, and the Big Flat property was ultimately transferred to the Montana Natural History Center for use in outdoor education.

In Missoula, both county and city governments were becoming fully engaged in the need to address growth and the changing landscape more actively. The Missoula City Council established a Conservation Committee to focus on these issues and develop plans and processes to address them. The first meeting was held in September of 1977, with Alderman Bill Boggs as chair. Over the coming months, in addition to discussing a variety of concerns, particularly energy conservation and drought, ideas began to circulate about ways to protect the scenic beauty of the Missoula Valley and other natural values not necessarily confined to the river and stream bottoms. Two Missoula landmarks, Mount Sentinel and Mount Jumbo, that stand above the Clark Fork River at the mouth of Hellgate Canyon, drew the committee's particular attention. Discussions began about the challenge of protecting their still-undeveloped flanks. Committee representatives began tentative discussions with several landowners on the two mountains.

As conservation efforts stepped up, so did tensions between conservationists and the industries that relied on natural resource extraction, particularly the timber and mining industries, which had long held sway over Montana's economy and politics. The Anaconda Copper Mining Company, with its massive mine in Butte, had become infamous during the first half of the twentieth century for its powerful, and monied, influence in the state Legislature and for control of much of the state's media, especially its newspapers. By the 1970s, "The Company" had faltered financially and its grip on state affairs had loosened. Nevertheless, resource extraction industries like mining and timber still powered much of the Montana economy and employed many Montanans. Publicly owned lands controlled by the USFS provided much of the timber that fed the state's wood products industry.

Against this backdrop, the future of nearby Rock Creek and its legendary trout fishery became a focus of nationwide interest, ultimately resulting in creation of the Rock Creek Trust, which would eventually figure large in the future work of FVRPA's successor organization.

In the 1970s and early 1980s, USFS' plans for logging in western Montana's Rock Creek watershed were met with broad concern and even outrage. Long recognized as the only "blue-ribbon" trout stream west of the Continental Divide in Montana (as designated by Montana FWP), Rock Creek had been a nationally known fishing destination since the early 1900s. Famous for its annual hatch of giant, orange-bodied stoneflies, or salmonflies, which drove trout crazy, the stream attracted anglers from across the country. This was years before Norman Maclean's classic, *A River Runs Through It,* became a significant factor in creating the billion-dollar fly fishing industry so important to Montana's economy today.

The public demanded a voice in USFS planning, resulting in raucous meetings that enflamed participants on all sides. The tension was eased somewhat by creation of a USFS advisory body of concerned citizens, industry representatives, and state and federal agency personnel called the Rock Creek Council. Ultimately, with agreement from the group, the USFS placed a moratorium on logging in the drainage. It was significant, not just for Rock Creek, but for resource planning across the board by government agencies in the decades to come. The public had demanded their voice be heard.

But battlelines had been drawn, too. Conservation advocates became known as "environmentalists," and the term was packed full of negative connotations for most people who relied on logging, mining, and related activities for their livelihoods. The resulting schism in society would never be completely mended, and it would take hard work to undo the mistrust each side developed for the other.

In Missoula, however, conservation-minded residents and public officials continued to look for ways to accommodate growth and protect the things that made Missoula a special place to live.

In December of 1978, the Missoula City Council approved a plan, proposed by Bill Boggs, to put a $500,000 bond on the spring election ballot for the purpose of purchasing land, or conservation easements on private parcels, on both Mount Sentinel and Mount Jumbo. Because of the usually poor voter turnout in spring elections, and the requirement that bond votes have at least 40% of registered voters participate, passage of the bond was a long shot. Though the bond was approved by a more than two-to-one margin, it failed for lack of turnout. This problem would resurface several more times in the years to follow, including the very next spring, when turnout was again too low for passage. Undaunted, Boggs soon announced plans to try to put the bond question before voters again, on the November 1980 ballot, a presidential election year likely to draw more than enough voters to the polls for bond approval.

Boggs was right, but it didn't happen without some controversy. In what *Missoulian* editorial page editor Sam Reynolds called, "the campaign's most tawdry cheap shot," the Missoula County commissioners campaigned against the bond. The commissioners claimed that zoning could be used to achieve the same goals without expense to the taxpayers. Reynolds pointed out the obvious–that zoning could be changed–and protection would never be guaranteed. The voters agreed with Reynolds. The bond passed in the same election that Ronald Reagan was elected president.

Over at Smitty's Pancake Parlor, it wasn't Smitty's anymore. Perkins Cake and Steak had taken over the Rattlesnake Creek-straddling restaurant. The special was breaded veal cutlets for $4.95. The 1980 census revealed another big jump in Missoula County population. The county was now home to 76,000 people.

Although passage of the bond issue was momentous for local conservationists, it was clearly overshadowed by President Jimmy Carter's signing of the Rattlesnake National Recreation Area and Wilderness Act of 1980 on October 21. This put under protection over 60,000 acres of the Rattlesnake Mountains and its alpine lakes, beginning just four miles from Missoula.

The campaign for wilderness designation had been in the works for years, promoted locally by a group called Friends of the Rattlesnake, with Missoula City Council member Cass Chinske as spokesman. This effort to protect the Rattlesnake had been the most visible local land conservation issue for some time. With broad local and national public support, along with the Wilderness Society, a national organization, and the Montana Wilderness Association, Montana's congressional delegation, Senators Max Baucus and John Melcher and Representative Pat Williams, had managed to secure congressional approval. It was a great victory for wilderness supporters, but it was not lost on observers that the new wilderness designation exacerbated the growing controversy around environmental protection.

Even so, as 1980 wound down, city voters had finally approved a $500,000 bond that would serve as a model for similar efforts in Missoula, and all across the Rocky Mountain West, in years to come. In February of 1981, the Missoula City Council created a new Open Space Advisory Committee to oversee bond expenditures and look for new ways to protect key open space lands.

With general community approval, the bond funds were ultimately directed at the three key elements of open space identified as priorities during the bond's campaign.

The funds were used to purchase a long-sought parcel along the recently defunct Milwaukee Railroad right-of-way on the south bank of the Clark Fork through downtown Missoula, between Higgins Avenue and Van Buren Street. Part of that acreage has since become John Toole Park and the hub of Missoula's riverfront trail system.

In addition, the City entered lengthy negotiations with the Dr. Walter Cox family, owners of a significant portion of the west-facing slopes of Mount Sentinel that look out over Missoula, for the protection of 300 acres adjacent to UM and USFS property. Deputy City Attorney Mae Nan Ellingson led the negotiations for the city, which resulted in the purchase of the easement in 1982 using open space bond funds.

This was the first parcel protected by a conservation easement in the Missoula Valley. The easement limited further development on the 300 acres. The City of Missoula held the easement, meaning the city became responsible for seeing that the restrictions on development were honored by the landowners.

Finally, in 1987, the city utilized bond funds to purchase 125 acres on the southwest face of Mount Jumbo, just north of the "L." Following that successful purchase, the Open Space Advisory Committee and local open space advocates continued to explore ways to protect the rest of the mountain. Their effort would have crucial ramifications for the future of conservation in the Five Valleys, and beyond.

While this acquisition work was being completed by the City of Missoula in the 1980s, it was not a time of feverish activity at FVRPA. There were too many other things going on that diverted the attention of members of the organization, such as continuing water and air quality degradation, timber harvest practices on public lands, and zoning and planning efforts amid rapid regional growth.

New advocacy groups had formed, or were about to form, to focus on broader landscape level issues. The Westslope Chapter of Trout Unlimited was established in Missoula out of concern for cold water fishery habitat in western Montana lakes and streams. The Clark Fork-Pend Oreille Coalition, now the Clark Fork Coalition, appeared in 1985 in response to increasing degradation of, and growing threats to, water and air quality in the entire Clark Fork watershed. The Rocky Mountain Elk Foundation emerged from a small group of Troy residents in 1984 with a focus on protection of elk habitat and ensuring and increasing public hunting access to those lands. The RMEF almost immediately experienced explosive growth, resulting in the relocation of its headquarters to Missoula in 1988, and would play an important role in the future of FVRPA in the years just ahead.

In the short-term, however, FVRPA's organizational activities had ground to a halt, even though its members were actively involved in many of the ongoing conservation initiatives and issues in the community and across Montana. In fact, one of those issues in particular created some spirited dissension among the organization's members. That was a proposal to construct an oil pipeline across the entire state, generally following the route of the now defunct Milwaukee Railroad, right through the middle of downtown Missoula. Called the Northern Tier Pipeline, it would have carried oil from Minnesota to Puget Sound. Some members thought it would be an economic benefit to the community, outweighing the obvious environmental concerns. Ultimately, concerns for the potential environmental impact to Puget Sound killed the proposal, but not before it created a schism among FVRPA members.

Early in the 1980s, Bob Knight, who had been seeing to it that FVRPA's nonprofit status was kept up to date, despite the inactivity, prevailed upon Helena Maclay, one of his partners in the Knight, Maclay & Maser law firm, to assume the role of keeping the organizational torch lit by attending to necessary annual reporting to the State of Montana and the Internal Revenue Service. Maclay dutifully saw to it that the legal bones of the organization remained intact.

Tension continued to mount between the advocates of development and resource extraction and the conservation community. Missoula had become something of a ground zero for those conflicts. In a September 23, 1980, *Missoulian* article, reporter Sherry Devlin wrote, "If you're looking for Environmental Battlefields 101, you've come to the right place. Missoula, as they say, is under siege."

WHAT IS A LAND TRUST?

A land trust is a non-profit organization that is authorized to work with private landowners to create legal agreements called conservation easements. A conservation easement is a voluntary legal agreement by which a landowner chooses to limit certain uses of his or her land in order to conserve some value it provides. For example, landowners may agree to limit or prohibit subdivision or construction of new residences on a parcel. Land placed into a conservation easement still belongs to the landowner, and the landowner retains the rights to sell the land or pass it on to heirs. Most landowners with conservation easements continue to live on and manage the land for farming, ranching, timber, recreation, and other uses.

Conservation easements are tailored to meet the needs and long-term goals of each landowner. The land trust that holds the easement is responsible for ensuring that the mutually agreed-upon terms and conditions of the conservation easement are honored and acts as a resource for landowners as they work toward these goals. Conservation easements are recorded documents and appear on the title just as road and utility easements do. They are legally binding, and they are perpetual.

In addition to working with individual landowners to protect private lands, a land trust can also act as a facilitator in situations where local, state, and federal governments are constrained from acting quickly to protect or acquire private lands for public ownership and use.

THREE

NORTH HILLS FOR SALE: BECOMING WESTERN MONTANA'S LAND TRUST

SIEGE OR NOT, CONSERVATION EFFORTS CONTINUED into the 1980s while discussions and disputes swirled around rapid growth, city annexation, and sewer expansion and who would pay for it. That's when it became known that the Montana Power Company was interested in divesting itself of over 400 acres in the Rattlesnake Valley and the North Hills of Missoula. Some of these lands lay within the high priority trail corridor that FVRPA had identified along Rattlesnake Creek.

A recurring theme in the history of FVRPA and its ultimate successor, Five Valleys Land Trust, has been the ability to recognize and capitalize on opportunities. This would prove to be one such pivotal moment. The effort to realize the vision of the Rattlesnake Greenway would eventually propel FVRPA into its next incarnation.

On Sunday, December 22, 1985, a *Missoulian* editorial, while outlining the challenges surrounding development of Montana Power Company lands in the Rattlesnake, quietly suggested that "Some of Montana Power's land along Rattlesnake Creek would make a magnificent park, similar in beauty and quality to Greenough Park downstream. Public officials and private citizens should be alert to that (some already are) and begin thinking about how to acquire the parkland. Where might the money come from? Who would lead the effort? Does it have wide community support? What kind of deal can be struck with Montana Power over the parkland? Lots of questions and few answers."

With Missoula County struggling to address the issues related to continuing rapid population growth and commercial and residential development, the county commissioners had been paying attention to the still somewhat embryonic land trust movement and began discussions about the possibility of helping create a community land trust for Missoula.

The county had already been looking for more tools to accomplish its land use and conservation goals and to incorporate environmental concerns into planning and zoning. In 1985, Missoula County hired Bruce A. Bugbee & Associates to compile its first "Inventory of Conservation Resources." This inventory included wildlife habitat, agricultural land, fisheries, recreation opportunities, scenic open space, and more throughout the county. Bugbee was also tasked with putting together a package of incentives that could prompt developers to consider protection of those conservation values in their projects, as well as providing incentives for private landowners to consider conservation.

Missoula County also assigned staff to the city's new Open Space Advisory Committee. Using the county's rural planning office to house it, the county created a new staff position for a natural resource specialist. Amy Eaton Royer, already a staff member, was assigned to the task in 1988. Eaton Royer credited the three County Commissioners, Anne Mary Dussault, Janet Stevens, and Barbara Evans, for giving her free rein to establish a local land trust.

"I feel very fortunate to have worked under that trio because they were an amazing group in getting things done and to look at new avenues to do it," Eaton Royer said in a 2023 interview.

That's about when Helena Maclay and Bob Knight stepped in with a "have we got a deal for you," suggestion. Still existing as a qualified 501(c)(3) organization, FVRPA could be reconstituted as a land trust by amending the original charter to assume the role and legal responsibilities of a qualified land trust.

After discussions among Missoula County officials and FVRPA representatives, which were spearheaded by the county through the efforts of Amy Eaton Royer, Five Valleys Land Trust (Five Valleys) was officially and very quietly created on April 17, 1989.

The mission statement for the revitalized organization was, "to protect for future generations western Montana's natural legacy–our river corridors, wildlife habitat, agricultural lands, and scenic open spaces."

Missoula County agreed to provide temporary office space, and Eaton Royer was designated as executive director–a half-time position–while continuing her duties with the county on a half-time basis. She was Five Valleys' first paid staffer, with Missoula County picking up the tab.

As with the original meeting of FVRPA, the first organizational meeting for the land trust drew something of an all-star cast of community members. At the first meeting, a new board was elected consisting of Arnold Bolle, FVRPA founding board member, former dean of UM School of Forestry, and President of The Wilderness Society; Ron Bender, a local attorney; Bob Burke, a Missoula banker; Betty duPont, retired rancher and conservationist; Robert Henry, local businessman; Randy Jacobs, former FVRPA board member and president of First National Bank; Hal Luttschwager, Missoula County insurance manager; Katherine Roush, landowner and conservationist; John Talbot, former publisher of the *Missoulian*; Dave Tawney, local dentist and conservationist; Chuck Tribe, Lolo National Forest planner; and Virginia Tribe, Lolo National Forest public affairs officer. Luttschwager was elected as the first board president of the new land trust. Betty duPont, John Talbot, and Chuck Tribe would all go on to serve continuously on the board for more than two decades.

"Group acts as conservation conduit" was the headline of a December 30, 1989, *Missoulian* article by Donna Syvertson announcing the young land trust's existence. This was almost nine months after the official creation of Five Valleys.

Missoula County Commissioner Ann Mary Dussault enthused about the prospects for the new community land trust and explained the county's decision to take part in its founding. In the same *Missoulian* article, she cited the challenges faced by government in dealing quickly with transactions involving private landowners and the reluctance of some private landowners to deal with the government in any form.

"I think it's one of the better things we've done in the last couple of years," Dussault proclaimed.

"One of the things I'm personally interested in, is making sure some of the mountainsides around Missoula don't get solidly developed," added founding board member John Talbot, foreshadowing the work to come.

New board president Luttschwager offered his own vision of a land trust that would respond to community needs, saying that Five Valleys "should do what the community wants it to do," adding, "we'll just have to see where it leads us."

As it happened, the Missoula community was providing some direction and the new land trust was already in the thick of efforts to acquire some of the Montana Power Company lands in the Rattlesnake Valley, as first suggested in that 1985 *Missoulian* editorial.

"Land trust bids for Rattlesnake property" was the headline of a companion story to the December 30, 1989, article announcing Five Valleys' creation. In her companion article, Syvertson made clear that the work before the fledgling Five Valleys included building community support and finding funding to purchase the Montana Power Company lands and create a greenway.

With many of the usual suspects working in the background–including Bob Knight, Bruce Bugbee, Amy Eaton Royer as the sole Five Valleys staffer, community members representing groups such as Friends of the Rattlesnake, and many, many others–an option-to-buy agreement was struck between the City of Missoula and Sunlight Development, a real estate subsidiary of Montana Power Company, to purchase Sunlight's lands for the Rattlesnake Greenway. Only those close to the action had any idea of the project's complexity or the human effort

An aerial view of the northwestern Rattlesnake Valley with the approximate Rattlesnake Greenway lands identified in orange. –*Photo by Jahrig Media, Five Valleys Land Trust collections.*

and behind-the-scenes work required to move such a project from the good idea stage to something that's ready to present to the public. Just how to get the next step–finding funds to complete the acquisition–accomplished was a work in progress as the 1980s were expiring.

That next step included Five Valleys assuming responsibility to organize and fundraise for the purchase of the Sunlight property. Ultimately, as a result of more complex negotiations, Five Valleys assumed the option agreement. The new land trust had already submitted a grant application requesting $633,000 from the federal Land and Water Conservation Fund to help with the 411-acre acquisition.

As the new decade dawned, Missoula Mayor Daniel Kemmis took the reins of a city coping with all that comes with rapid growth, including the Rattlesnake Greenway project. The county population reached 79,000, according to the 1990 census. The restaurant over Rattlesnake Creek had morphed again. Now it was known as Finnegan's Family Restaurant. Breaded veal cutlets were no longer on the menu. A family-style meatloaf dinner, going for $6.95, was now a popular entrée. And the city had fully entered another period of wide public concern and involvement in local government's approach to restoring or protecting the natural values that are so much a part of Missoula's community identity.

"We have to treat open space as infrastructure," proclaimed Mayor Kemmis in a June 14, 1992, *Missoulian* article, espousing his conviction that, "Open space is a positive value of central importance to the Missoula way of life. We want to look across the valley and see green."

Amy Eaton Royer had plunged into the job as Five Valleys' executive director with tremendous enthusiasm, working to build community support for the Rattlesnake purchase, while also raising funds to support the operation of the land trust in its own right. Securing federal funding for local projects requires serious political action, which in turn requires an outpouring of public interest and enthusiasm. Eaton Royer and Five Valleys Board members and supporters went about the task with a zeal that would set the standard for many of the projects that would come down the line in the years ahead. Senator Max Baucus, who was personally committed to the Rattlesnake Greenway project from the beginning, and the rest of the Montana congressional delegation responded by gathering support among their colleagues in Congress. As with all good things where the federal government and Congress in particular are involved, nothing happens overnight. But the effort was gathering momentum, steadily creating more and more community engagement.

Big milestones were afoot, however. During this early period of the land trust, Eaton Royer was spending time meeting and educating local landowners on the potential benefits and intricacies of protecting cherished private lands with conservation easements. The first two conservation easements donated to Five Valleys were officially finalized on December 28, 1990. Working with landowner Horizon Enterprises Inc., the easements protected two parcels off Grant Creek Road near the intersection with Snow Bowl Road, one 2 acres in size and the other 21 acres. The legal aspects of the transactions and the drafting of the conservation easement deeds were handled by the Knight, Maclay & Maser law firm. Eaton Royer contracted with two UM environmental studies graduate

Five Valleys' first conservation easements, located in Grant Creek northwest of Missoula, were finalized in 1990. *–Five Valleys Land Trust collections.*

students to complete a biological, human, and historical inventory, or "baseline report," for each property. A crucial step in the conservation easement process, baseline reports document the natural values that justify the conservation easement as well as provide a benchmark to refer to when overseeing the easement through the decades.

With the acceptance of these two Grant Creek easements, Eaton Royer and the Five Valleys Board of Directors recognized that their role had expanded far beyond the early aspirations of FVRPA, beyond the Rattlesnake land and the local stream corridors, and now encompassed the entire Missoula Valley. Conservation success on that scale would require a whole new level of community and local government involvement, as well as a spirit of collaboration among conservation groups and natural resource agencies. To that end, Eaton Royer and a group of community conservation leaders gathered to launch an initiative to foster that cooperative spirit. It came to be called "Land and Water for Wildlife."

Montana FWP, the Lolo National Forest, Rocky Mountain Elk Foundation, Montana Cooperative Wildlife Research Unit, the City of Missoula, and Missoula County all agreed to participate with Five Valleys as a strategic planning group. Land and Water for Wildlife had an overarching goal of protecting the wildland-urban interface and the rich habitat and resources that sustained the wildlife around Missoula. In particular, the group focused its attention on the elk herds that frequented Mount Jumbo, Grant Creek, the North Hills, and the Blue Mountain/O'Brien Creek areas. Meeting monthly, the group exchanged information on conservation opportunities that might arise, presented updates on current activities, and provided support and critical review of each other's efforts.

It was clear to all that funds would need to be raised to accomplish much of the conservation work the group had envisioned. And so, a modest fundraising campaign was launched. Mary Beth Percival, a local artist, agreed to create a poster to depict the wildlife and landscape in a way that encapsulated the vision of the group. The result, entitled "Living on the Edge," was a beautiful, iconic creation that depicted elk walking down a wildflower filled hillside and served to highlight the special values that grace the Missoula Valley. The print was made available for sale, with proceeds funding activities related to the overall goals of Land and Water for Wildlife. Like many of her husband Monte Dolack's posters,

"Living on the Edge" by Mary Beth Percival.
–Image courtesy of Monte Dolack and Monte Dolack Fine Art.

Percival's work is cherished and displayed in homes all around and far beyond western Montana today.

With Eaton Royer's leadership, Five Valleys had organized a tremendous show of support for the Rattlesnake Greenway project, by holding public informational meetings and community tours and launching an exhaustive letter writing campaign to Montana's delegation and the Congress. The project needed congressional support to complete the purchase of the Sunlight Development property by the City of Missoula.

Closing the deal, however, was not without some blood, sweat, and tears. Five Valleys and Rattlesnake Greenway supporters were ready to celebrate in November of 1990, when Congress approved a Land and Water Conservation Fund appropriation for the purchase, only to discover certain thorny legal issues would delay the project. Undeterred, project facilitators got back to work. These included Eaton Royer, Five Valleys Board members, a loyal advisory group, countless members of the broader Missoula community, and tireless efforts by Senator Max Baucus and Congressman Pat Williams, along with the determined work of Bob Knight. The federal appropriation that allowed the city to acquire the greenway finally came through in early 1991. In March, Mayor Kemmis, authorized by the City Council, signed the closing documents that sealed the deal.

This time, the celebration really came to pass. On September 14, 1991, a gala event was held in Pineview Park, adjacent to the new Rattlesnake Greenway.

With the Rattlesnake Greenway completed, Five Valleys was deemed ready to fledge. Missoula County stepped away from funding staff and providing office space. A new office was established in one of the rooms in the basement of the historic C. P. Higgins Building on the corner of Higgins and Main Streets. The office,

From left: Senator Max Baucus, Five Valleys Executive Director Amy Eaton Royer, a young supporter, and Nevada Senator Harry Reid at the "Rally for the Rattlesnake Greenway," September 1990. *–Five Valleys Land Trust collections.*

From left: FVRPA founding member Helen Bolle, Five Valleys Executive Director Amy Eaton Royer, and Five Valleys Board President Hal Luttschwager at the "Rally for the Rattlesnake Greenway," September 1990. *–Five Valleys Land Trust collections.*

not much larger than a phone booth, or so it seemed, housed a desk, an electric typewriter, a telephone, and a two-drawer filing cabinet. Now, for the first time, Five Valleys needed to pay rent, a phone bill, and a salary to keep the organization going.

Bob Knight and Jim Masar at Pineview Park during the Rattlesnake Greenway celebration, September 1991. *–Five Valleys Land Trust collections.*

In early 1992, Eaton Royer announced plans to move on to a new professional opportunity as Glacier-Flathead Director for the Montana Land Reliance, where she would serve with great success for many years. She agreed to stay on until December 1992, when Tracy Stone-Manning was hired to take her place, just as Five Valleys turned its attention to Mount Jumbo and other key conservation lands in the valley.

The board soon recognized the need for a more structured organization and wasted little time in creating a committee system aimed at addressing the future needs that were now so apparent. The original committees included a stewardship and management committee, a fundraising committee, a personnel and finance committee, a nominating committee, and an executive committee.

In addition, the board, at the urging of Chuck Tribe in particular, began developing a compendium of standards and practices to guide the daily operations of the organization. These were based on the recommended standards and practices developed by the Land Trust Alliance, a new national organization promoting business-like and ethical operations of land trusts across the country. Originally founded as the Land Trust Exchange in 1982, the Land Trust Alliance was organized "exclusively for the benefit of ... publicly supported local, state and regional private and public organizations that are engaged in land and related natural resource conservation." It remains so today.

Tracy Stone-Manning, bringing conservation experience from the Craighead Wildlife-Wildlands Institute, Defenders of Wildlife, and the National Wildlife

Federation as its representative on the Rock Creek Advisory Council, was well equipped for the job.

In short order, Stone-Manning shepherded the organization's third conservation easement into its final stages. Bill Randolph Jr., who had lived his entire life on a small farm in the North Hills to the west of the Rattlesnake Valley, wanted the land to remain open and in agricultural use after his death. The property had begun as a 160-acre homestead farmed by Ray and Luella Moon. In 1907, the homestead was purchased by Bill Sr. and Emma Randolph, who used their highly diversified, farmstead that included laying hens, dairy and beef cattle, vegetables, honey, and an apple orchard to get their family through the Great Depression.

Attorney Jim Maser represented Bill Randolph Jr. in the matter, as he would for a number of conservation easement donors in years to come. Five Valleys' third easement was finalized in December 1992. Today, the property is owned by the City of Missoula as the Moon-Randolph Homestead, and is managed for natural history and agricultural education, as well as for recreational use via a trail system. Five Valleys continues to hold the conservation easement.

During this period, and at Chuck Tribe's insistence, the board and newly designated stewardship and management committee began to seriously address the organization's stewardship responsibility. As a land trust, Five Valleys assumes an additional legal responsibility with each new conservation easement to assure the requirements, restrictions, and management practices agreed upon with landowners–known as easement grantors–are faithfully observed and carried out. The accepted standard is to visit each easement annually to assure the terms are being met. This is a perpetual responsibility, and must be faithfully accomplished by the land trust, as grantee. This annual visit is referred to as an easement monitoring visit.

Fundamental to good stewardship of conservation easements is the maintenance of a good working relationship between the land trust and easement landowners. The annual monitoring visits are the primary tool for developing and maintaining those relationships. But the land trust's obligations don't stop there. Often, landowners have challenges with management involving a whole variety of issues such as noxious weeds, forest insect outbreaks, riparian fencing, general range and forest management, and any number of other, often unforeseen management challenges. The land trust can serve as a conduit for natural resource information, sometimes lending the hands of staff or volunteers toward addressing an issue. With a handful of conservation easements to steward, the challenge in those early years was not daunting. Later on, however, it would become a significant element of the daily work of Five Valleys.

It also became apparent early on, both to staff and the board of Five Valleys, that one of the greatest pleasures of doing conservation work would be the personal relationships that developed with those landowners who shared in the love of place, the land, and the natural world so fundamental to the conservation work of Five Valleys. Over years, many of those professional relationships would develop into lifetime friendships.

Adding to the stewardship responsibilities of Five Valleys, Stone-Manning quietly completed Five Valleys' first conservation easements in Pattee Canyon with Jeannette and David Tawney and Nancy and Ron Erickson in 1993. These were simple easements, preventing further subdivision and residential construction, while protecting habitat and traditional agricultural uses. As with most of the early easement efforts, they were generously donated by landowners who wanted future generations to experience and enjoy the landscape and the flora and fauna as they had. These two early projects would lay the foundation for significant conservation work in Pattee Canyon and on Mount Dean Stone in the decades to come.

Helen and Arnold Bolle, circa 1992. *-Photo courtesy of the Montana Outdoor Hall of Fame.*

As these efforts were taking place, a pall was cast over the work. Arnold Bolle, a founding member of FVRPA and Five Valleys and a giant in the local and national conservation community, passed away in March 1994. He had been an inspiration for so many of those who shared his vision and benefited from his humanity.

Alongside conserving private properties with conservation easements, Stone-Manning

Aerial view of Mount Jumbo, looking south down the Rattlesnake Valley circa 1990.
–*Five Valleys Land Trust collections.*

continued with the Land and Water for Wildlife initiative. A major focus continued to be the fate of private lands on Mount Jumbo that were now more and more likely to become available for purchase on the open market. Stone-Manning initiated discussions with several of the landowners on the mountain, one of whom suggested an attractive alternative could be to open a restaurant on its summit. Although few took the suggestion seriously, it was clear that public acquisition of the mountain would be the only way to prevent haphazard development. Further evidence of the imminent threat to the mountain was the existence of a billiards table-sized, three-dimensional model of Mount Jumbo used in a subdivision proposal. One hundred tiny cardboard houses filled the saddle area, spilling up the sides of the model's slopes.

Knowing significant funding challenges would make any effort to protect Jumbo a daunting task, Stone-Manning sought support from local government to once again put an open space bond initiative before Missoula County voters. Around the time those discussions were getting underway, a new group, Save

Open Space, emerged with the stated intent of providing more focus on protecting urban open space within the community, rather than on the wildland-urban interface. A lively exchange followed among one of the founders of the group, Andy Sponseller, a local welding contractor, and Richard Gotshalk, Chair of the city's Open Space Advisory Committee. The groups were able to settle their differences on how bond money should be spent and gained the support of the city and county to place an $8 million bond issue on the June 1994 election ballot. The two organizations worked together in hopes of securing passage of the initiative.

"People really are concerned that things are spiraling out of control," Stone-Manning told *Missoulian* reporter Sherry Devlin in a May 29, 1994, article about the bond election. "We have to shape what our communities look like before they are shaped for us. I really believe that our responsibility as citizens is to make sure we don't roll over the natural world. Ultimately, it's the right thing to do, for ourselves and for other creatures, too."

On election night, it appeared to all that the open space bond had passed with room to spare. However, it was determined that a number of voters had not chosen to vote one way or another on the issue; they had simply left that blank on their ballots. The specter of the same technicality that had doomed the open space bond initiatives of 1978 and 1979 rose from the ashes. For passage, a certain percentage of qualified voters must participate in any bond issue election. Although more than enough voters voted in the election, a significant number of voters failed to choose at all, meaning their ballots did not count as part of the total required for passage. Even if the non-voters had all voted against the bond, it would have still passed. But that didn't figure into the Missoula County Attorney's decision that the bond had not met the letter of the law for passage. The thrill of the perceived victory on election night was gone. All parties resolved to try again in that fall's general election.

Soon after the June 1994 election, Stone-Manning tendered her resignation. Stone-Manning would go on to have a long and successful career in conservation, later becoming the director of the federal Bureau of Lands Management.

Greg Tollefson, local outdoor writer and conservationist, was hired to fill the vacancy at Five Valleys. His background in conservation work included private environmental consulting and serving on the Montana Legislature's Environmental Quality Council, the State Council of Montana Trout Unlimited, and as chair of the Rock Creek Advisory Council. Tollefson's experience with the Rock

Creek Advisory Council had focused heavily on using conservation easements to achieve meaningful natural resource protection in the watershed.

Given full leeway on how to use the funds designated for a modest salary, one of Tollefson's first decisions was to hire Minie Smith as Five Valleys' first stewardship director. Minie Smith had worked with The Nature Conservancy in Maine before relocating to Missoula and earning her graduate degree in UM's Environmental Studies program. She was to share the already growing load of work stemming from increasing interest in conservation easements. For the first year, both directors–presumably directors of each other–shared one salary while working full-time for Five Valleys. And Five Valleys unveiled its brand-new logo in the fall newsletter of 1994.

The first logo of Five Valleys Land Trust.
–Five Valleys Land Trust collections.

The marching orders provided to Tollefson were short and sweet. "We want you to continue to work with private landowners to protect important lands with conservation easements," Five Valleys Board President Chuck Tribe instructed. "And we want you to work to save Mount Jumbo."

Elk wintering on a protected Mount Jumbo. *–Photo by Paul Queneau.*

FOUR

THEN CAME MOUNT JUMBO

IT WAS A DAUNTING TASK, not only for Five Valleys, but for anyone who seriously contemplated preserving Mount Jumbo in its semi-wild, undeveloped state.

Its summit rises 1,500 feet above the Missoula Valley floor, well above the shoreline of ancient Glacial Lake Missoula, and sprawls over approximately 2,800 acres.

In addition to its imposing beauty, Mount Jumbo also happened to provide critical winter range for a herd of elk, somewhere between of 80 to 100 strong. Every year, the elk arrived as winter closed in and spent the long cold months browsing on the lush grasses of the open south-facing slopes. To lose Mount Jumbo would be catastrophic for that elk herd. And something wild and priceless would be lost to everyone in the community.

But how do you go about "saving" something so enormous?

From the outset, everyone involved–Five Valleys, local government, other conservation organizations, and countless individuals who threw themselves into the task–realized the only way it could possibly happen was through a coordinated, community-wide effort.

Meanwhile, Five Valleys itself was ramping up. A symbolic moment occurred when board member Betty duPont provided Five Valleys with its first timid step into the world of technology with the gift of a retired Apple Macintosh computer. Not long after that, the office typewriter began to collect dust.

Very quickly, Five Valleys was again involved in promoting a Missoula County open space bond request, this one scheduled for the November 1994 general election. Once more, Five Valleys and representatives from Save Open

Space and Missoula County's Open Lands Citizen Advisory Committee faced the looming job of convincing voters to support an open space bond. But this time, there was a new challenge.

The wording on the ballot did not make it clear that the bond would be for open space in particular. It was instead referred to as a "general obligation bond." Only by reading the small print would voters be able to discern its true purpose. For legal and technical reasons, by the time the wording was identified as a problem, it was too late to change the ballots.

To compound the issue, little funding was available in the fall of 1994 to launch a serious public relations and education campaign in support of the bond. So the relatively small group of supporters did their best with presentations to community groups, handing out explanatory fliers, and cobbling together several short, home-cooked ads for television. One memorable ad featured Sander Tollefson, Greg Tollefson's 7-year-old son, standing forlornly along the side of a road near the Clark Fork River bottom, outfitted with his fishing gear, against the backdrop of a busy residential construction project between road and river. The recording no longer exists, and one can only guess that the message was something along the lines of, "If you want to be sure your kids will get to enjoy the outdoors like you do, support the open space bond." Amateur all the way.

Concerns about the confusing ballot language turned out to be justified. Voters soundly defeated the well-disguised open space bond. Many who voted in the election expressed surprise that the open space bond issue didn't seem to be on the ballot at all. But disappointment at the failure of the open space vote didn't last long.

Discussions with Mount Jumbo landowners were progressing very slowly. During the same period, new inquiries about conservation easements were coming into the tiny Five Valleys office daily. Five Valleys' small staff and active board responded to landowners' information requests, moved ahead with prospects that looked promising, and began working with developers in the North Hills in an effort to dispel the notion that Five Valleys was somehow anti-development. The board wanted the message to be, "We aren't anti-development, we're pro-conservation."

That winter, recognizing the need to bolster capacity amid growing demands on the organization, the board decided it was time to hold a fundraising banquet.

They did so with a dinner and auction at the Elks Club on Front Street in downtown Missoula.

However, it was not generally understood that a buffet was involved. So, after a cocktail hour, the fifty or so guests were all seated and waiting politely to be served. One of the caterers approached board member and banquet committee chair Tom France at the head table and whispered in his ear. A look of concern flashed across Tom's face and he rose to his feet, walked to the lectern, adjusted the microphone, and announced with a sweeping gesture toward serving tables along one wall, "Ladies and gentlemen, it's a buffet!"

The auction followed, with Gary Wolfe, president of the Rocky Mountain Elk Foundation, as auctioneer. Helen Bolle, who had participated in the first FVRPA meeting offered up one of her famous huckleberry pies, and it turned out to be a big-ticket item. Over the next decade of banquets, Helen Bolle's pies would bring wildly exorbitant bids in the name of conservation. The final item that came up for bid that night, somewhat unexpectedly, was Tollefson's gaudy red tie emblazoned with a jumping trout. It brought in $300.

That evening was the beginning of the annual tradition of Five Valleys' banquet and auction. The banquet would grow into a much-anticipated spring event that would regularly sell out tickets to 500 or more people, one of the largest such events in the region. Usually held in May just as the arrowleaf balsamroot was blooming, the banquet would come to engage wide swaths of the community through business sponsorships, a great diversity of donated auction items, and tireless volunteerism. Importantly, the banquet would celebrate conservation and help raise the funds necessary to advance Five Valleys' efforts.

WHILE FIVE VALLEYS WAS GAINING TRACTION AS A REINVIGORATED CONSERVATION GROUP, both local governments continued with plans to address growth and protection of important conservation lands from a regulatory standpoint. Kate Supplee had been hired to staff the City Citizens Advisory Committee on Open Space, which was about to complete a Missoula Urban Area Open Space Plan. The plan was intended to identify and prioritize "open space cornerstones," those features in the valley that were most important to protect from development, and what

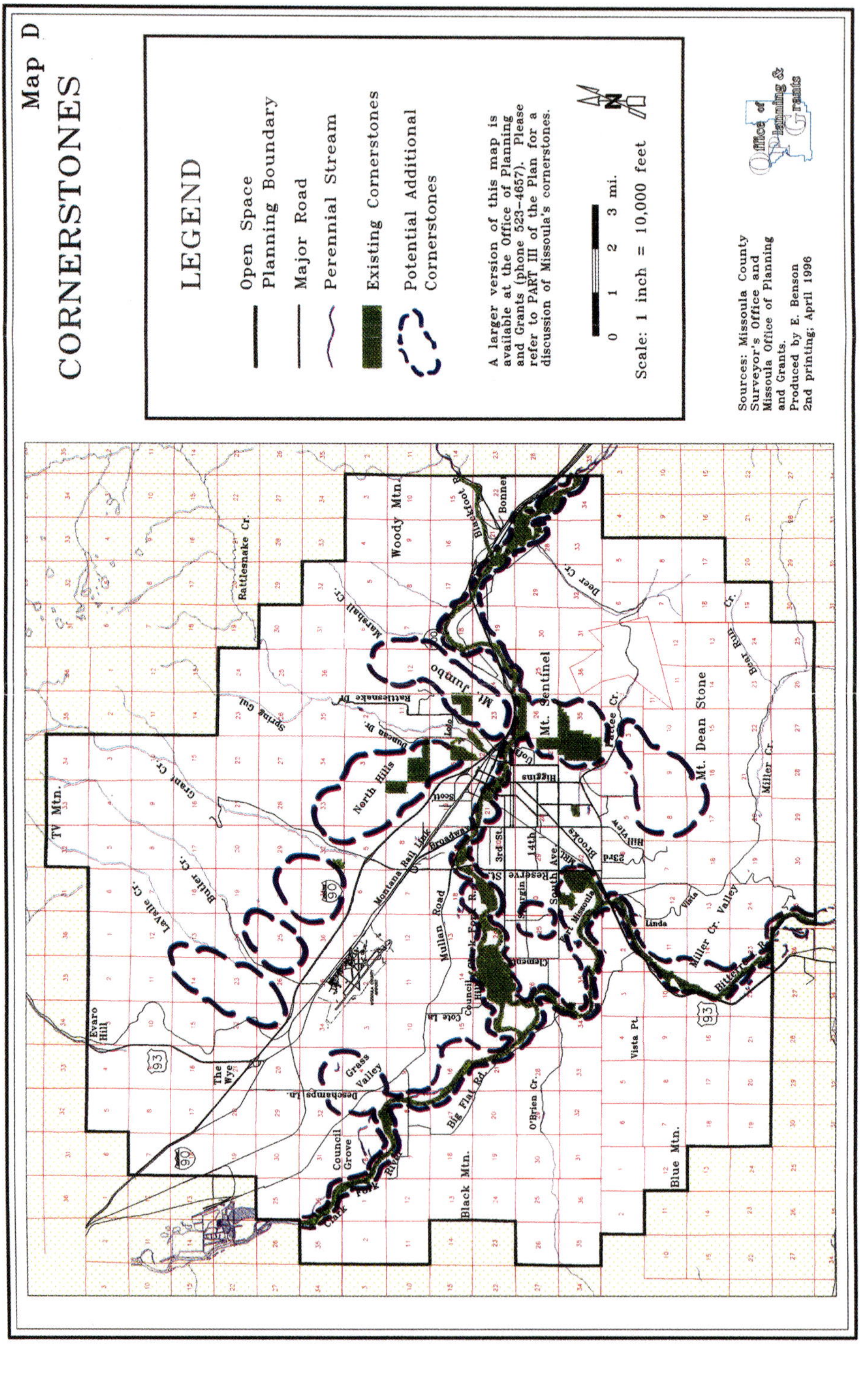
Map D
CORNERSTONES
LEGEND
Open Space Planning Boundary
Major Road
Perennial Stream
Existing Cornerstones
Potential Additional Cornerstones
A larger version of this map is available at the Office of Planning and Grants (phone 523-4657). Please refer to PART III of the Plan for a discussion of Missoula's cornerstones.
0 1 2 3 mi.
Scale: 1 inch = 10,000 feet
Sources: Missoula County Surveyor's Office and Missoula Office of Planning and Grants.
Produced by E. Benson
2nd printing; April 1996

kind of protection would be most suitable. In some cases, that could mean important scenic values might best be safeguarded with conservation easements that left the views intact and historic agricultural uses in place while remaining in private ownership. Other lands with significant scenic values, but also great potential as public recreational lands, could be identified as priorities for public acquisition as the best way to assure protection and a variety of uses.

In June of 1995, the Open Space Advisory Committee unveiled the Missoula Urban Area Open Space Plan. As expected, the vital open space cornerstones included Mount Jumbo, Mount Sentinel, Mount Dean Stone, the North Hills, McCauley Butte, and the stream corridors that vein the Missoula Valley. Mount Jumbo was singled out for its unmistakable scenic value, its importance as critical winter range for elk and other wildlife, and for its potential as a public recreational resource. And there was a growing urgency about Mount Jumbo–the looming knowledge that portions of the mountain were at risk of development.

When things started to happen regarding Mount Jumbo, they happened quickly. Interest in protecting the open space cornerstones was growing throughout the community. Then, the largest landowner on the mountain, John Klapwyk, passed away. Now Five Valleys had the opportunity to launch a campaign to protect Mount Jumbo through public acquisition.

Representatives of the estate of John Klapwyk knew of Five Valleys' interest. They came forward with an offer to sell the property at fair market value. The price tag, however, would be steep for a small community land trust with few financial resources: approximately $2.75 million. Attorney Harry Haines, representing the Klapwyk estate, and Bob Knight representing Five Valleys, began negotiations.

For Five Valleys, it represented a challenge that was difficult to grasp. With landowner permission, Board President Chuck Tribe and Tollefson hiked to the northernmost high point on the mountain on a beautiful spring day to weigh the options for the organization over a leisurely lunch. That was the moment, looking out over the mountain and the valley below, when Tribe turned to Tollefson with his conclusion.

"We don't have a choice here," he said. "We have to do this."

Opposite: Missoula's open space cornerstones as first identified in the 1995 Missoula Urban Area Open Space Plan. *–City of Missoula Office of Planning and Grants.*

Although it may have taken a little more detailed discussion to come to the same conclusion, the Five Valleys Board, with a collective sigh at the thought of the challenge ahead, agreed to enter into a purchase option for the Klapwyk property. On June 2, 1995, Tribe signed the option agreement on behalf of Five Valleys. The option came with a price. With only $500 in the till at Five Valleys, the Rocky Mountain Elk Foundation, active participants in the Land and Water for Wildlife initiative, came to the rescue with $4,500 to secure the $5,000 purchase option. Now there was no turning back.

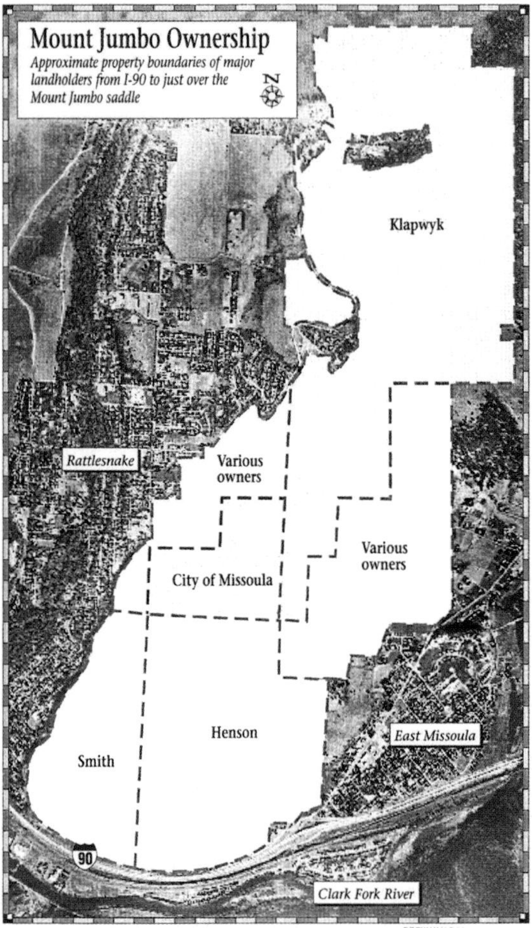

A map of parcel ownership on Mount Jumbo in 1995. – *Drew Van Fossen,* Missoulian *archives.*

What followed proved to be a transformative experience for Five Valleys as an organization, and for the community at large, as they grew to understand and embrace the importance of key open spaces that shape community identity, afford all manner of recreational activities, provide habitat for a wide variety of plant and animal species, and grace us all with natural beauty.

In addition to the Klapwyk property, several other landowners held title to the contiguous open space that made up the bulk of the mountain. Each of those landowners would have to agree to sell. It took several years to bring together all of the partners and funding needed to get it done, ultimately $3.2 million. But for starters, Missoulians at last had a project in place that could be partly funded by an open space bond.

The Open Space Advisory Committee, now chaired by UM professor Ron Erickson, Mayor Kemmis, and the City Council, as well as County Commissioners Ann Mary Dussault, Fern Hart, and Barbara Evans, all endorsed putting a $5 million open space bond issue on the ballot. So did Save Open Space and a number of other community organizations. This time there would be a clear target for some of the bond money. But all parties also agreed the bond must be planned to address multiple open space concerns, not just Mount Jumbo.

Mount Jumbo supporters faced a multi-pronged challenge. A bond issue of approximately $2 million would be required to pay for a big hunk of Mount Jumbo. Given the demoralizing defeats of previous bond requests, they knew a real campaign was essential to pass a bond issue. It would take money to do that. There would also have to be a continuing fundraising effort to secure the remainder of the money needed to purchase all the critical properties on the mountain.

A campaign committee was essential. A campaign director would be needed. Five Valleys agreed to provide office space and act as fiscal agent for a campaign. Local political organizer Jim Parker was hired to run it.

The Five Valleys Board quickly realized that the two-person staff could not handle daily duties, including the necessary real estate transactions, if they were also deeply involved in the people management necessary to carry out a bond campaign. It was also obvious that the tiny Five Valleys office was inadequate to deal with the level of activity that lay ahead.

Noreen Humes was hired to help with the logistics of the Jumbo campaign. This freed up time for Tollefson and Smith to attend to project details and ongoing conservation efforts with private landowners around the county. It didn't take long for Humes' new job to evolve into a more general office management position.

As luck would have it, office space became available immediately adjacent to Five Valleys' subterranean office, providing lots more area for Humes to oversee. The change more than quadrupled the space available for the campaign and the years ahead. Five Valleys never looked back.

The funding scheme for the $3.2 million required to protect Jumbo would not be simple. Success of the bond campaign was not a given. Even if the bond

The 1995 Five Valleys Land Trust staff. From left: Minie Smith, Greg Tollefson, Ellen Knight, and Noreen Humes. *–Five Valleys Land Trust collections.*

measure was successful and $2 million was earmarked for Jumbo, raising another $1.2 million would be daunting.

Senator Baucus, whose support had been crucial in securing funding for the Rattlesnake Greenway, would again be key to accessing federal support through the Land and Water Conservation Fund. The Rocky Mountain Elk Foundation was a phenomenal local partner, providing the earnest money needed to secure the purchase option, as well as literally thousands of volunteer hours from staff members and thousands more dollars of incidental cash contributions to the campaign. Particularly meaningful was a $10,000 contribution from the Percy Phillips Memorial Fund, administered by the Rocky Mountain Elk Foundation. Percy Phillips was an East Missoula teenager who perished tragically in an avalanche on Mount Jumbo in January 1993. The Montana chapter of The Nature Conservancy provided crucial financial help with a loan at a pivotal moment in the process. The USFS, Montana FWP, and the City of Missoula using open space funds, all played major roles in the ultimate success of the effort. So did a number of private foundations, and generous major individual donors.

However, the true shining stars of the effort to acquire Mount Jumbo for the public were the hundreds of Missoula citizens who responded to the challenge. The first public organizational meeting for the campaign was held at the Rocky Mountain Elk Foundation office, then located on West Broadway. Tollefson, nervous before the meeting, had the misfortune of experiencing a double spontaneous nosebleed driving to the event. Introducing himself to start the meeting, he stood before more than 100 community members with two giant, walrus-like tusks of tissue dangling from his nostrils. It proved to be a good ice breaker and didn't deter those in attendance from beginning the hard work of creating what nearly became something that qualified as a social movement before all was said and done.

The entire community was energized by the prospect of buying Mount Jumbo for the public. Neighborhood groups formed to raise money. Volunteers flooded into the small Five Valleys office wanting to know how they could help. A twenty-member fundraising committee representing every imaginable social and political niche in town rolled up its sleeves and went right to work.

One group prepared a slideshow with an accompanying script and made copies, then rounded up a dozen slide projectors. Board members and community volunteers lined up for an opportunity to pack a projector to meeting after meeting of any community group that expressed an interest, to spread the Mount Jumbo gospel. Demand for showings at public and private schools, churches, service organizations, and UM remained steady for months.

Also in great demand were volunteer-led hikes on the mountain. Peter Lesica, local botanist and the compiler of definitive publications on the flora of Montana, gave his time for highly popular wildflower and botanizing walks. Will Kerling, a longtime advocate for conservation of Jumbo and the Rattlesnake Valley, led butterfly expeditions. Bob Henderson, Montana FWP wildlife biologist for the Missoula area, led groups interested in wildlife, particularly the elk herd that relied on the mountain for winter range. So did Gary Wolfe, president of the Rocky Mountain Elk Foundation, who along with many Rocky Mountain Elk Foundation staff, simply led groups up the mountain to talk about the overall project, and especially the elk.

Several strategically located businesses erected billboard-sized thermometers showing the progress of fundraising, inching higher and higher. Lemonade stands and bake sales cropped up all over town in support of the campaign. Local photographer Nelson Kenter donated a classically beautiful photo of Mount Jumbo that was used to create a poster to raise funds. Kids emptied their piggy banks and proudly brought handfuls of change into the Five Valleys office. Rattlesnake Valley resident and Save Open Space Board member Janet Sproull exemplified many supporters who tirelessly campaigned for Jumbo, volunteering at every opportunity, organizing events, writing letters to the editor, lobbying local and state officials, and generally spreading enthusiasm for the project. Another notable example, Tony Veazey, a longtime Missoula and western Montana businessman and community leader who had grown up in the Rattlesnake Valley, successfully secured significant contributions from all the one-time holders of irrigation water rights for the historic Rattlesnake Ditch. Veazey, a mining engineer by education, had worked much of his life in extractive industries, including

Nelson Kenter's signature photo of Mount Jumbo that was used in the fundraising campaign. –*Photo by Nelson Kenter, Five Valleys Land Trust collections.*

Bob Henderson, Montana FWP wildlife biologist, and Chuck Tribe, Five Valleys Board President, at the closing celebration for Mount Jumbo, March 1997. *–Five Valleys Land Trust collections.*

managing the Anaconda Mill in Bonner. His enthusiasm for the Mount Jumbo project provided an inspiring example of the way shared values and love of place transcend the somewhat artificial barriers that can get in the way of so much that Montanans from all walks of life cherish in common. The same could be said for so many supporters who made the project into a personal quest, and donated time, money, and great energy to the dream of community ownership of the mountain.

Most local elected officials voiced their support. So did many professional groups. Yellow "Save Mount Jumbo" change jars cropped up next to cash registers in businesses around town. Mount Jumbo bumper stickers and coffee mugs were snapped up as quickly as they arrived and spread around town like knapweed. T-shirts and sweatshirts appeared, emblazoned with "Save Mount Jumbo" and "Vote Open Space." A group of artists organized by poet Sheryl Noethe put together a CD of music and poetry called *The Stories Project-Jumbo Love Cycle* to raise money for the mountain. At Lewis and Clark Elementary, as part of a schoolwide study of Lewis and Clark, each classroom created and auctioned off large papier-mâché sculptures of wildlife observed on the Voyage of Discovery, with the proceeds dedicated to Mount Jumbo. The western tanager created by Maureen Kane's multi-age class is still on display somewhere in the Five Valleys office.

The Jumbo campaign truly became a community campaign.

When Election Day, November 7, 1995, dawned, a cold wind was spilling out of Hellgate Canyon. Mixed rain and snow continued for most of the day. Undaunted, Missoula voters turned out in droves to overwhelmingly pass the

$5 million open space bond.

"Open Space, Yes!" read the oversized banner headline in the following morning's *Missoulian.* As the sun rose, a large smiley face, fashioned from bedsheets and visible for miles, appeared high on the south slope of Mount Jumbo.

A campaign ad asking for loose change for Mount Jumbo, 1995. *–Five Valleys Land Trust collections.*

Passage of the open space bond issue was a giant step toward acquiring Mount Jumbo. But there was still a long and winding road of fundraising and land transactions ahead for Five Valleys, its partners, and the community. The campaign went on, and the totals in the billboard thermometers kept creeping upward. Little by little, transactions were completed and more of the mountain moved into public ownership. The final significant portion of funding was $250,000 from the federal Land and Water Conservation Fund, sought and won by Senator Baucus and announced October 31, 1996.

The final documents were signed, and new deeds recorded on March 27, 1997. The *Missoulian* headline the next day read, "Jumbo is ours!"

That announcement was just in time for the Five Valleys spring banquet and celebration of the twenty-fifth anniversary of the founding of FVRPA. The anniversary was also noted in a feature story in the *Missoulian* on March 30, with a companion story about Five Valleys' first conservation easement donation in Mineral County, completed in partnership with the Jan and Dick Roberts family.

By the time the dust settled and the last document had been signed, the Mount Jumbo campaign had become more than a local project. Contributions had been received from individuals, foundations, businesses, and other groups from thirty-nine different states and four Canadian provinces. Contributions came from more than 1,300 individuals, 350 businesses and community groups, and a number of local and national foundations.

As might be expected, Bob Knight was once again integral to the success of the Mount Jumbo campaign, providing guidance, negotiating purchase agreements, handling all of the complicated legal work, and quietly fundraising. Ellen Knight, busy with conservation in Rock Creek, nevertheless played a vital role by enthusiastically generating public support and searching high and low for sources of financial support. It had been two decades since Bob and Ellen attended the first FVRPA meeting, and they hadn't missed a beat.

A smiley face made of bedsheets on Mount Jumbo the morning after the passage of the 1995 open space bond. *–Photo by Michael Gallacher.*

A time lapse photo of Rock Creek. *–Five Valleys Land Trust collections.*

FIVE

FROM POWERLINES TO PRESERVATION: THE ROCK CREEK TRUST STORY

THE SUCCESS OF THE MOUNT JUMBO CAMPAIGN brought Five Valleys new visibility and credibility as an important civic partner. Staff were soon fielding calls from other Montana cities, and even Salt Lake City and Boise, for advice on how to successfully engage a community and generate support for the new idea of open space bonding. Another new era had begun.

By the time the Mount Jumbo purchase was completed and the land was transferred to the City of Missoula, the USFS, and Montana FWP, the land trust was actively negotiating and accepting new conservation easements and working hard at educating landowners about the ways an easement might serve their conservation purposes, as well as their financial planning needs.

This growing interest created a demand for increased capacity within the organization. Hence the decision to make the spring banquet an annual affair. Five Valleys also launched a development program to expand its funding base and establish itself as a membership organization. Noreen Humes was tapped to serve as the first development director.

Thus far, the work of the land trust had been focused exclusively on the Missoula Valley. More and more often, however, landowners from outlying areas were knocking on the door, interested in conservation easements.

The first major step into the world of conservation work beyond the confines of the Missoula Valley came in 1995, when the organization known as the Rock Creek Trust approached Five Valleys. The Rock Creek Trust, with its single full-time staff person, Ellen Knight, and a substantial pool of financial resources, had built a track record of accomplishing good conservation work.

Members of the Rock Creek Advisory Council at Hogback Cabin in 1993. From left: Rich Clough, Montana FWP representative; Jim Posewitz, Montana FWP representative; Greg Tollefson, Westslope Chapter of Trout Unlimited representative, outdoor writer, and future Five Valleys Land Trust executive director; Tracy Stone-Manning, Five Valleys Land Trust executive director and National Wildlife Federation representative; Art Compton, Montana Department of Natural Resources and Conservation representative; Ellen Knight, Rock Creek Trust Director; Chris Marchion, Montana Wildlife Federation representative. *–Five Valleys Land Trust collections.*

Knight, of course, was one of the twenty folks who attended that first FVRPA meeting in 1972 and was the wife of FVRPA and early Five Valleys attorney Bob Knight. The story of Ellen Knight and the Rock Creek Trust's efforts remains as consequential to Rock Creek as the FVRPA was to Missoula.

Nearly a decade earlier, in 1985, Montana FWP, the Westslope Chapter of Trout Unlimited, the National Wildlife Federation, and the Montana Wildlife Federation filed suit over a permit granted to the Montana Power Company and the Bonneville Power Administration for a 500kv power line that was to extend from

Garrison to Thompson Falls. The route cut an 80-foot-wide swath along the entirety of its path, which included a crossing five miles above the mouth of Rock Creek.

The plaintiffs contended that the environmental assessment and planned mitigation measures were inadequate. The lawsuit was settled with the creation of a $1.65 million trust fund, the Rock Creek Trust, and a quasi-governmental advisory body that would assume the name of the old Rock Creek Advisory Council. Because Rock Creek was recognized as a unique and biologically rich natural feature that would be significantly impacted by the proposal, it was determined that the funds could best be used to engage in activities that would serve to safeguard the natural resources and values that made Rock Creek a natural, and national, treasure.

The Montana Board of Natural Resources was designated as trustee for the fund and given oversight of expenditures. But projects would be identified and carried out by the new Rock Creek Advisory Council, made up of representatives from the Westslope Chapter of Trout Unlimited, the National Wildlife Federation and the Montana Wildlife Federation, Montana FWP, the Montana Department of Natural Resources, and Rock Creek landowners.

The group began meeting in 1986. The first order of business was to craft a mission statement:

> *The Rock Creek Trust is dedicated to protecting and enhancing Rock Creek's famous "Blue Ribbon" trout waters, the health of its nationally acclaimed wildlife habitat, its unusual biodiversity, and the open space beauty of the drainage. Specifically, the Council seeks to protect open space on key parcels of private land through the use of conservation easements and other land protection tools, and to help protect water quality and wildlife habitat through cooperative projects with landowners, agencies, or other organizations. The Council seeks to accomplish these conservation goals before growing pressures cause irreversible damage in this treasured drainage.*

The logo of the Rock Creek Trust. –*Five Valleys Land Trust collections.*

Soon thereafter, the Rock Creek Advisory Council issued a request for proposals from groups and individuals interested in projects that would achieve the mission. Early on, funding was provided for a number of projects proposed in response to that general solicitation. What follows is a partial list of projects and activities funded in part, or entirely through the Rock Creek Trust:

- Water quality monitoring in Rock Creek and its tributaries by the USFS.
- Construction of an interpretive trail at the Valley of the Moon by Montana FWP and the USFS.
- Stream rehabilitation in Gilbert Creek with a private landowner.
- Dust abatement on Rock Creek Road in Granite County.
- Restoration of the Historic Hogback Cabin with the USFS.
- Writing and publication of the local history, *Up the Creek: History of Early Settlers on Rock Creek, Bonita, and Quigley* by Darlene Olson, in 1990.
- Funding of a Lions Club youth summer camp on Rock Creek.
- Publication of the resource management history, *For the Sake of the Creek: Land and Water Use in the Rock Creek Basin & the Effort to Preserve the Resource* by Margaret Knox, consultant to Montana Watercourse, a Bozeman firm, in 1991.
- A study of *Pteronarcys californica* (giant salmonfly) by the University of Montana.
- A study of groundwater/nutrient load by the University of Montana.
- Funding for noxious weed control by the Rock Creek Weed Board.
- Major stream channel restoration efforts by the USFS.
- An East Fork Dam Failure Warning Plan by Rock Creek Protective Association.
- And many other projects.

Yet, it was becoming clear that the single greatest threat to the health and vitality of Rock Creek was residential development. With its spectacular views, world-class fishing, and short commute to Missoula, Rock Creek was a coveted place for a weekend cabin. Growth was especially concerning along the narrow stream corridor in the lower drainage nearer to where the creek empties into the Clark Fork, as well as among the historic cattle ranching community in the broad upper valleys along Rock Creek's west, middle, and east forks. Larger properties were often subdivided in 5-acre parcels, threatening the ecology and character of the watershed.

With the City of Missoula and Five Valleys having both put conservation easements to recent use, there was a growing awareness of how easements could benefit both the land and landowner. This led the Rock Creek Advisory Council to focus on working with willing private landowners to achieve a mutual vision for the future of Rock Creek. What followed was a combination of projects involving donated conservation easements, purchased conservation easements, land exchanges, purchase and resale of high priority lands with easements or other protection in place, and activities designed to further protect and enhance lands already secured with easements.

In an interview in 2022 about her time with the Rock Creek Trust, the FVRPA, and Five Valleys, Ellen Knight had this to say:

> *When I was working in Rock Creek, there were two challenges that I particularly worked with and one of them was working with landowners, the ranchers up in the upper end and the others in the lower end. I was concerned as a woman about having credibility in a world that was mostly men. The fishermen and the hunters were mostly men. I thought, I'm not a hunter, I'm not a fisherman. But I absolutely loved aquatic insects. I thought, I will just have to be myself. I didn't try to be anybody I wasn't, and I tried to be honest and thoughtful. And it worked well.*
>
> *The other challenge was trying to meet people and talk to them about conservation easements. That's a challenge in itself. There was a lot of diversity in the landowners in the drainage. People in lower Rock Creek didn't have the same kinds of questions, usually, as the upper Rock Creek landowners. People did not know what conservation easements were, and so that was one of my goals, to help people understand them and help them see how it might be beneficial to them. Certainly, most of them had a sense about the creek and the land–they loved it, you know–so there was a connection there whether, they wanted an easement or not.*

At the urging of Governor Marc Racicot, the State of Montana relinquished its trustee role and allowed the Rock Creek Advisory Council to become a wholly non-governmental body in 1995. This would allow the council fewer procedural hurdles and more efficient use of trust funds.

The newly emancipated Rock Creek Advisory Council considered many new avenues, including becoming a stand-alone non-profit. After considering the council's new focus on conservation easements, their complementary missions and adjacent landscape, the Rock Creek Council approached Five Valleys about merging with the land trust. The Rock Creek Trust became a "special project" of Five Valleys Land Trust in September 1995.

"We're a good match," Board President Chuck Tribe told the *Missoulian* on October 1, 1995, announcing the merger. Ellen Knight agreed, adding, "There's a shared wisdom that we benefit from–and new efficiencies and flexibility."

Prior to 1995, all easements negotiated by Rock Creek Trust were held by Montana Land Reliance. After the merger, new easements were held by Five Valleys.

The Rock Creek Advisory Council continued to serve as an advisory body, recommending expenditures of the remaining trust funds to the Five Valleys Board of Directors.

Together under Knight's leadership, the Rock Creek Advisory Council and Five Valleys forged ahead in their work. The effort attracted diverse funders and partners, including the Westslope Chapter of Trout Unlimited, National Trout Unlimited, the Montana Natural Resource Damage Claim Program, Montana FWP, private foundations including the Liz Claiborne Art Ortenberg Foundation, the Charles Engelhard Foundation, the Foundation for North American Wild Sheep, and charitable donations from the Rock Creek landowners who granted easements and made the work possible. Perhaps most crucial was the partnership that slowly developed with a group of Rock Creek landowners who organized into the Rock Creek Protective Association, giving a true community voice to discussions around resource use and protection in the precious Rock Creek watershed.

The Rock Creek Trust's legacy is the leveraging of the original $1.65 million fund many times over and the protection of nearly 13,000 acres and more than 20 miles of stream frontage. Based on appraisals conducted for properties at the time, the Rock Creek Trust's work exceeded $20,000,000 worth of conservation value. With the escalation in land values over the years, that figure would translate to considerably more today. Rock Creek continues to be a high priority area for Five Valleys, who holds thirteen Rock Creek Trust easements and will do so in perpetuity.

In 2012, after twenty-six years, the Rock Creek Trust would complete its final project. That year, the remaining trust funds would be committed to yet another pivotal project, at the confluence of Rock Creek and the Clark Fork River, that would change the course of how Five Valleys would serve its growing community.

Rock Creek, near the confluence of the Clark Fork River. *–Photo by Little Bear Photography, Five Valleys Land Trust collections.*

FIVE VALLEYS LAND TRUST SERVICE AREA

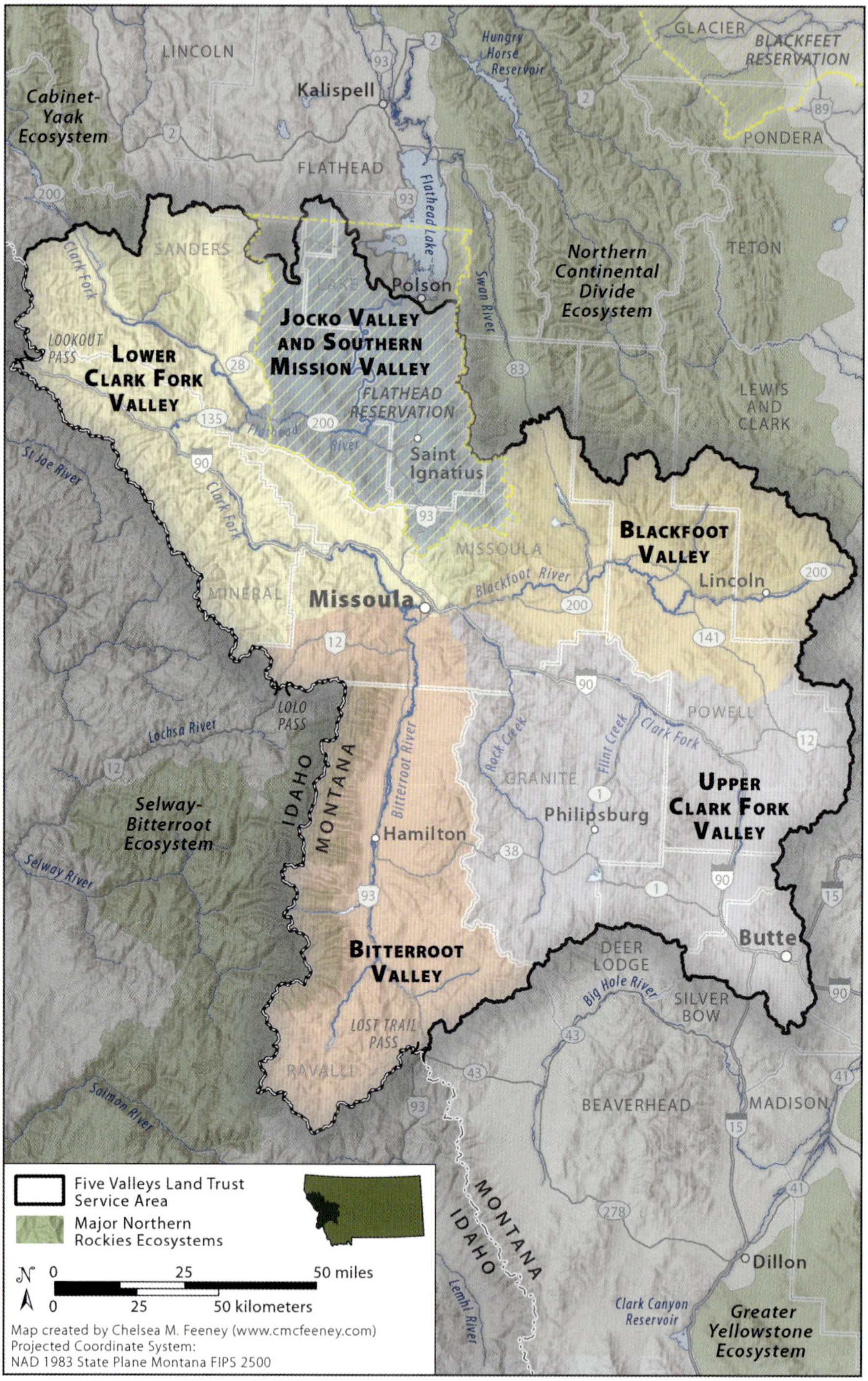

SIX

THE GREAT LEAP FORWARD AND OUTWARD

EVEN AS THE ROCK CREEK TRUST MERGER WAS TAKING PLACE and the Mount Jumbo campaign was ongoing, Five Valleys had already begun to operate on a new level. The organization's four staff members, now including Ellen Knight as the Rock Creek Trust director, were regularly negotiating and accepting new conservation easements on private lands.

That, in turn, led to more project inquiries from landowners.

The fourteen easements completed by Five Valleys in 1997 ranged from upper Rock Creek in Granite County, to the confluence of the Clark Fork with the Flathead River in Sanders County, to Ravalli County in the Bitterroot Valley, to Oregon Gulch near Superior in Mineral County. And what became known as the Five Valleys service area was beginning to look as if it could truly reflect the Five Great Valleys.

As Five Valleys staff, board members, and supporters know, each one of those conservation easement projects represents a story of individuals and families who cherish their relationships with the landscape and share a vision for the future of those places that recognizes a responsibility to keep natural systems intact and natural beauty unblemished. Five Valleys staff learned early on that the relationships they established with conservation-minded landowners were an important part of the reward of land protection efforts. Those trusting and respectful relationships are the rock-solid foundation of land trust work.

Just such a relationship among land, landowners, and the land trust was beautifully demonstrated in a letter from Dick and Jan Roberts, donors of Five Valleys' first conservation easement in Mineral County, a beautiful parcel of old-growth cedar and rich riparian habitat in Oregon Gulch:

We like to fancy that the trees and all that grows on our land thank us for protection long after we are gone, that all the animals living here and those who visit have a future safe from human domination. Nature will take its course here with as little interference from humans as can possibly be assured. We're convinced there must be areas to be left undeveloped, unexploited. The land trust gives us this assurance.

Jan and Dick Roberts on their property in Oregon Gulch, 2007. *–Five Valleys Land Trust collections.*

Now, with a growing number of conservation easements requiring land trust oversight, the organization began to develop a stewardship program that could respond thoroughly to the responsibilities that come with perpetual easements.

Jim Berkey, who authored one of the first stewardship procedures manuals available nationally, contracted with Five Valleys to handle the annual easement stewardship program that had been initiated by Minie Smith. As with many contractors and volunteers who have passed through the doors of Five Valleys, Berkey would eventually make himself invaluable and become a full-time employee with much broader responsibilities.

Five Valleys also created a Stewardship and Conservation Committee comprised of board members and staff, as well as community members, to provide counsel, approval, or review of ongoing and proposed projects. Chuck Tribe, a founding board member and former Five Valleys Board president, served on this committee from its inception through his retirement from the board in 2016. His leadership and insistence on adherence to a required set of standards and practices and policy development has had a lasting impact on the quality of the work accomplished by Five Valleys.

The Stewardship and Conservation Committee continues to work with Five Valleys staff to handle sometimes thorny compliance issues. As a result, Five Valleys enters into easements with confidence in the organizational ability to honor the commitments assumed in those easements.

As 1997 came to a close, and with Five Valleys looking to new challenges and continued growth, both Greg Tollefson and Minie Smith chose to move on to new endeavors in conservation. Wendy Ninteman was named executive director. Known locally for her time as a Missoula television news anchor, Ninteman was also a former co-owner and manager of an environmental consulting firm, and former director of the resource management division of UM's continuing education department.

Ninteman inherited management of a land trust that now had the perpetual legal responsibility to monitor compliance for twenty-nine conservation easements spanning over 3,500 acres and four counties.

DESPITE ITS GROWING FOOTPRINT, THE PROSPECT OF DOING WORK BEYOND the Missoula Valley had been a contentious issue for the Five Valleys Board, generally based on concerns about organizational capacity and the need to attend to existing stewardship obligations. The inspiration provided by the successful Mount Jumbo campaign, however, sparked a growing feeling that the organization should broaden its view of where good conservation work could and should be undertaken. The Rock Creek Trust merger nudged Five Valleys toward this broader vision, and a growing staff allowed for "missionary" work in unserved western Montana counties. Over the next few years, the organization took on greater and greater challenges, and met them all.

Under the leadership of Ninteman, Five Valleys experienced a period of dramatic growth, both in capacity and in achievement. Ninteman succeeded in shaping Five Valleys into a smooth-running organization, upgrading technology, organizational outreach, and creating a number of board committees to support and advise the various necessary organizational functions. She worked with the national organization, the Land Trust Alliance, to assure that Five Valleys developed policies and procedures that thoroughly reflected the operating standards

active role in Five Valleys and local conservation work, and specifically agricultural land conservation, for the next quarter century. Not long after the Cusker family donated the easement on their property, Jim joined the Five Valleys Board of Directors and would serve there, with distinction, for many years.

Continuing to grow and to demonstrate a successful formula for landscape conservation, Five Valleys was now being noticed across the State of Montana. In the winter of 1998, the Montana Chapter of The Wildlife Society bestowed its Wildlife Conservation Award on the organization.

"To date, this small, locally based land trust is directly responsible for protecting over 10,000 acres of wildlife habitat," said Montana FWP biologist Bob Henderson at the award presentation. "In so doing, Five Valleys has become one of the most credible voices for conservation in Missoula and western Montana. We owe a lot to the people at Five Valleys, not only for what they have accomplished, but also for providing an example to follow."

The 1999 Five Valleys Land Trust logo.
–Five Valleys Land Trust collections.

That next year, 1999, Five Valleys debuted a new logo. This iteration's hand and five fingers reflected the Five Great Valleys that the organization now fully represented.

Also in 1999, Five Valleys joined a massive effort to protect and make public thousands of acres of prime wildlife habitat in the Blackfoot-Clearwater watershed. A half century prior, the State of Montana had bought a 67,000-acre ranch near the southern flank of the Bob Marshall Wilderness. Game managers at the time counted less than 100 elk on the property. The tract, known as the Blackfoot-Clearwater Wildlife Management Area (BCWMA), was managed by Montana FWP. Yet only around 25% of the property was public, threatening the long-term viability of the area for elk and other wildlife.

To ensure wildlife could continue to thrive, a coalition of conservation organizations including Montana FWP, the Rocky Mountain Elk Foundation, Five Valleys, and the Blackfoot-Clearwater Wildlife Management Area Citizens Advisory Council came together to raise $2.2 million to buy 7,800 acres within the management area from Plum Creek Timber Company. Monte Dolack was commissioned to create a fiftieth anniversary painting that could be used to promote the project. The image, an instant Dolack classic, was made into posters and sold for $30 each out of the Five Valleys office.

Today, the BCWMA provides critical winter range for elk and other wildlife and remains a special place where current and future generations can connect to the landscape.

"Blackfoot- Clearwater" by Monte Dolack. *–Image courtesy of Monte Dolack Fine Art.*

By the new millennium, the pace of population growth and residential and commercial development had increased dramatically. The 2000 census found almost 96,000 residents in Missoula County, an increase of 22% in just ten years. At Five Valleys, the ongoing challenge was staying ahead of, or at least keeping up with, the growth and the threats to the landscape, wildlife, water, agriculture, and recreational opportunities that such growth brings. The meatloaf dinner at Finnegans was still reasonable though, coming in at $8.95.

Key to keeping up was adding capacity, a euphemism for staff. In 2000, Jim Berkey became a full-time employee responsible for both easement stewardship and working with prospective landowners to negotiate new easements.

The other side of the capacity coin is made most evident when an inspirational and stalwart conservationist steps away after many years of loyal and historically significant conservation work. Ellen Knight made her graceful exit at the end of 2000. She left a legacy that continues to benefit all, and all those yet to come. Ellen did not leave conservation, however; she just shifted her focus to work in conservation education. Not only did she leave her mark among the founders of FVRPA and as the first and only staffer of the Rock Creek Trust, she also facilitated the seamless merging of the Rock Creek work with the ongoing work of Five Valleys. At the same time, she was among the founders of the Montana Natural History Center.

One important factor in the growing interest in and acceptance of the concept of private land conservation was the availability of funds remaining from the 1995 Missoula County open space bond. This resource provided an inducement for landowners whose financial needs sometimes precluded their ability to make blanket charitable contributions of the value in their family lands.

Five Valleys staff and supporters came to understand that protecting agricultural land and assuring continued agricultural use was becoming more important by the day, as much productive agricultural land was being converted to residential development.

Adjusting to personnel changes and shifting workloads, Five Valleys had begun reaching out to farmers and ranchers in the Potomac Valley up the Blackfoot as well as in the Grass Valley, just west of Missoula. Many of the conservation easements that resulted were made possible only by finding ways to fund the purchase of those easements.

Following the lead of several federal agencies in funding protection of agricultural values, riparian corridors, and critical habitat for protected species and others, Five Valleys worked to secure the funds remaining from the 1995 Missoula County open space bond for conservation easement purchases around the Missoula and Potomac Valleys. Those dollars have been leveraged and leveraged again by foundation grants, private donations, and multiple agency funding packages cobbled together by Five Valleys staff. Through the 1990s, staff became experts at creating financial packages that satisfied the needs and goals of landowners, funding agencies and organizations, the Five Valleys' mission, and the hopes of the many community members who have generously supported the work.

As Five Valleys grew, so did the necessity–and opportunity–to collaborate with like-minded groups. Five Valleys began working with members of the Blackfoot Challenge, a grassroots organization focused on protecting the agricultural heritage of the Big Blackfoot watershed. Their work would go on to create a conservation legacy that has become a model for rural conservation in the West.

Five Valleys' partnership with the Blackfoot Challenge turned out to be a productive experience, as well as a time of continued education. To work successfully with the agricultural community, Five Valleys staff learned to listen closely and look at the issues from the viewpoint of those whose livelihood depends upon the continued productivity of the land.

Together with The Nature Conservancy, Montana FWP, the US Fish and Wildlife Service, and other partners, Five Valleys participated in, and continues to participate in, creative conservation projects involving such disparate concerns as endangered species protection, establishment of public access, and stream restoration. During the first decade of this effort in the Blackfoot, Five Valleys was a partner in the protection of over 16,000 acres there, including twenty-one conservation easements.

The Upper Clark Fork was another important component of the growing Five Valleys service area. As it became apparent that there was lots of interest in conservation from the agricultural community of the Upper Clark Fork, the organization began to focus more on education and outreach. The region also energized the many Five Valleys supporters who valued the wildlife habitat, waterways, and beauty that the Upper Clark Fork provides. Five Valleys' first conservation easement in Powell County was completed in 2000.

A few years later, Five Valleys started working with one of the Upper Clark Fork's largest landowners, the Rock Creek Cattle Company. Not to be confused with the Rock Creek in Granite County and the Rock Creek Trust, the Rock Creek of the Rock Creek Cattle Company flows into the Clark Fork River in Powell County. By 2011, over 6,300 acres of Rock Creek Cattle Company land would be protected by four separate easements.

The Rock Creek Cattle Company property. *–Five Valleys Land Trust collections.*

AS MORE AND MORE PRIVATE LAND WAS PROTECTED WITH EASEMENTS, there arose new opportunities to engage supporters in events that would come to be known as "stewardship work parties." Quite often, such opportunities were the result of conversations with easement landowners who, in consultation with Five Valleys' staff, identified activities that might serve to restore or improve habitat or simply improve the health of the property. Loyal supporters were ready to pitch in to plant willows along a stream, restore or replace fencing, hold mass weed pulls, and help with unexpected chores that required more help than was immediately available at the farm or ranch. Five Valleys saw these activities as a logical extension of the trusting relationships it worked to build with conservation-minded landowners.

Around that time, the Perelman family became new conservation easement landowners near Ovando. Jill Perelman, her son, Kent Perelman, and her daughter-in-law, Mary Shaffer, had recently purchased the historic Copenhaver Ranch, now renamed the Sundance Ranch. After meeting with Ninteman, Jill completed a conservation easement with Five Valleys in December 2000 that protected 680 acres. It was Five Valleys' third-largest conservation easement at the time. Kent and Mary would follow suit, protecting another 70 acres of the ranch in 2003.

Earlier that year, in the summer of 2000, Montana FWP fisheries biologist David Schmetterling captured a westslope cutthroat trout in the Clark Fork River just below Milltown Dam. After outfitting it with a radio transmitter, the trout was released upstream of the dam where it swam more than 70 miles, first up the Big Blackfoot to the North Fork of the Blackfoot, then into Rock Creek (not, of course, the same Rock Creek as the renowned stream flowing out of the Sapphires), and finally into Dry Creek, a spring-fed tributary on the Sundance. The trout's monumental migration, which was detailed in the October 12, 2000, edition of the *Missoulian*, showed that the Blackfoot Valley watershed, while fragmented by the dam, still remembered itself.

Soon after purchasing the ranch, the Perelmans joined a local effort to restore riparian habitat along Rock Creek and its tributaries, Dry Creek and Salmon Creek, which had been badly degraded by poor land stewardship.

Working with the USDA Natural Resources Conservation Service, Montana FWP, The Nature Conservancy, the Big Blackfoot Chapter of Trout Unlimited, the US Fish and Wildlife Service, Greenwing Restoration LLC, the Montana Department of Natural Resources and Conservation, and Five Valleys, the Perelmans planted nearly 10,000 shrubs, trees, and cuttings along 14,500 feet of streambank. These young plants would require regular watering and monitoring year after year to ensure survival.

Once the planting was done, Five Valleys' then stewardship manager, Grant Bronk, recruited volunteers to pitch in. For the next decade, hundreds of volunteers, students, and Montana Conservation Corps members would drive up Highway 200 a few times each season to water seedlings and maintain the wire browsing protectors that guarded them. From that effort, Five Valleys' volunteer stewardship program, Hands on the Land, was born.

The tradition of cooperating with private landowners in this way has served to broaden community understanding of Five Valleys' work, at the same time that it solidifies relationships with those landowners. The popular program continues today.

Hands on the Land volunteers on the Sundance Ranch. *–Five Valleys Land Trust collections.*

The Cox property on the backside of Mount Sentinel. *–Photo by Mark Wilson, Five Valleys Land Trust collections.*

SEVEN

ANOTHER MOUNTAIN FOR MISSOULA

STANDING WATCH OVER HELLGATE CANYON opposite Mount Jumbo, Mount Sentinel stands as a true open space cornerstone. The mountain is perhaps Missoula's most recognizable landmark, due to the bright white "M" emblazoned on its northwestern flank, directly above UM's campus.

Many times, when a community, agency, or local group decides future generations would be well-served by the protection of a particular parcel of open space, the only way to secure it is to buy it.

Witness Five Valleys' previous work to help acquire lands near Missoula for the City of Missoula and state and federal agencies. The greatest barrier to these efforts is always money, but the next challenge is the time it takes to complete a real estate transaction by a public entity. The bureaucratic challenges can be so time consuming that a prospective seller is unable or unwilling to wait. Private entities, like land trusts, do not have the challenge and complexity of rule-driven public processes that can take weeks or years.

The flexibility to act quickly has enabled Five Valleys to facilitate important public acquisitions. The commitment necessary in such transactions is oftentimes huge, and risky, but more often than not, Five Valleys has been up to the challenge when the need is great and the danger of losing a valuable natural resource parcel is imminent.

Most often, these projects turn out to be multi-year undertakings, requiring significant fundraising efforts, local government, state or federal approval, huge amounts of staff time, multiple partnerships, a tremendous amount of voluntary legal expertise, and, of course, broad public support.

Mount Sentinel, like Mount Jumbo, towers over the Missoula Valley, inviting generations of Missoulians to climb the zigzag trail to the "M" and perhaps to visit the public lands farther east toward University Mountain. Funds from the first Missoula County open space bond in 1980 had purchased a conservation easement from the Walter and Evelyn Cox family, protecting 300 acres on the west face of the mountain, adjacent to UM and USFS lands. However, the remainder of the Cox family lands were unprotected.

Over the years, Five Valleys had stayed in touch with the Cox family, even after they had departed Missoula. With the passing of their parents and all the children living elsewhere in the country, the entire 950 acres of family land on the west and south slopes of the mountain became available for sale and was likely to be given over to residential development unless a community effort to acquire the land could be launched.

The Cox family was eager to work with Five Valleys, hoping they would not eventually have to sell the family lands to private interests. Ninteman worked tirelessly with the family for some time to negotiate a purchase agreement that both parties found acceptable. On August 21, 1999, Ninteman and the Cox family announced that Five Valleys had signed an option to purchase the nearly 1,000-acre property on the mountain.

In fairly short order, with strong backing from the general public, Missoula Mayor Mike Kadas, the city's Open Space Advisory Committee, the City Council with special support from council member Chris Gingerelli whose University Area district directly bordered the mountain, a portion of the 1995 open space bond was allocated to the purchase. On April 4, 2000, in exchange for $175,000 in bond funds, the city acquired 474 acres on the west slope of Sentinel, above the UM golf course.

In her *Missoulian* account the next day, reporter Sherry Devlin echoed her lead from the Mount Jumbo closing:

"Mount Sentinel is ours," she wrote.

Mayor Kadas extolled the importance of the open space lands that provide the boundaries of our community.

"When we see these hills, coming in by air or on the highway, looking up from our morning coffee, we remember who we are ... we stop as a city at this boundary," Kadas said.

Tom Cox, representing the Cox family, spoke of how fortunate he and his siblings were to grow up on the property and how pleased the family was to work with the community.

"It was a wonderful place. It still is," Cox said.

Chuck Tribe, speaking for the Five Valleys Board, praised the community effort. "This is such a fine example of cooperation between private landowners, government and a conservation organization. We need to protect these important landscapes that help to define our community. Now, the bookends of historic Hellgate Canyon are preserved," he said.

When it was her turn to speak, Ninteman joined in the celebratory feel of the day, but also reminded those in attendance that there was more work ahead to secure the remaining 476 acres of Cox land on the south-facing slopes of Mount Sentinel, above Pattee Canyon. She suggested a variety of alternatives were being considered, including the possible division and private sale of the land to conservation buyers who would commit to very limited development and conservation easement protection on the parcels. That would have been the quickest, and perhaps the easiest, way. But that's not what happened.

The remaining Cox family land above Pattee Canyon held so much potential for increased habitat conservation, recreational opportunity, incredible scenic beauty, and connection to USFS lands, including the Pattee Canyon Recreation Area, that public acquisition seemed critical. Ninteman continued discussions with the Missoula Ranger District and Lolo National Forest, as well as the City of Missoula, brought in members of Montana's congressional delegation, and accepted an offer of assistance from the Trust for Public Land, a national organization. When it appeared possible that Land and Water Conservation Funds could be accessed via the Lolo National Forest, with prodding from Montana senators and representatives, the City of Missoula agreed to allocate another $100,000 of open space money to the project. The Cox family agreed to extend the option period to accommodate the federal funding process.

As with previous public acquisition projects, countless community members pitched in to assure the effort would be successful. Local artist Kendahl Jan Jubb created two beautiful watercolors to promote the acquisition. Open space advocate and Five Valleys supporter Ethel MacDonald helped organize a Hidden Treasure Run on Mount Sentinel to build enthusiasm for the public purchase and introduce many of the participants to the beauty and natural diversity of open slopes and wooded draws on Mount Sentinel's "backside." Nearly 300 people joined in the adventure, some walking, some running, but all thoroughly enjoying the experience.

Longtime board member John Talbot wearing a tee shirt with the image of Kendahl Jan Jubb's watercolor "Celebrate Mount Sentinel," at the Hidden Treasure Run, April 2002. *–Five Valleys Land Trust collections.*

Once again, the broader Missoula conservation community and many recreational groups worked tirelessly to help secure federal funding. The support of Deputy Regional Forester Kathy McAllister, Lolo Forest Supervisor Debbie Austin and Missoula District Ranger Don Carroll was essential. So was start-to-finish support from Missoula Mayor Mike Kadas and Missoula Open Space Coordinator Kate Supplee. The usual letter writing to influential members of Congress was required. Community leaders and citizens appealed to Senators Max Baucus and Conrad Burns for their support.

The *Missoulian* announced the imminent closing of the deal on July 9, 2003. This time, the celebration did not come with caveats. The deeds changed hands,

Mount Sentinel conservation partners. From left: Five Valleys Land Trust Executive Director Wendy Ninteman, Missoula Mayor Mike Kadas, Missoula Open Space Coordinator Kate Supplee, Lolo National Forest Supervisor Debbie Austin, and Missoula District Ranger Don Carroll, 2003. *–Photo by Michael Gallacher.*

and the City of Missoula and the USFS took ownership of the mountain. Ninteman breathed a deep sigh of relief. She expressed gratitude to the Cox family for their patience with the long process, and to all the supporters who, with dogged determination, made sure the Mount Sentinel purchase would succeed. Her summation of the project was brief.

"This property is one of Missoula's most spectacular open space gems," she said.

It remains so today.

Ninteman's work on the Sentinel project–determined, imaginative, and collaborative–set the tone for the rest of her tenure at Five Valleys and solidified the organization's status as a forward-looking community institution.

While the Sentinel acquisition was underway, the day-to-day work of the organization continued apace. As had become increasingly clear over the years, the completion of a major project, though a cause for celebration, did not mean Five Valleys staff could sit back and bask in the accomplishment. There is always another opportunity or challenge waiting to be addressed.

Five Valleys Land Trust strategic planning session, 2003. From left, Tom Demmons, Jim Cusker, Betty duPont, Scott Hollenbeck, Chuck Tribe, Gary Wolfe, Susan Maser, Anne Boone, Marcia Hogan John Talbot, Amber Sherrill, Rod Triepke, Kristine Beal, Bob Whaley, Tom France, and Gary Burnett. *–Five Valleys Land Trust collections.*

To meet those challenges, Ninteman and the Five Valleys Board continued to cultivate support, both from the community at large and from an ever-expanding network of private funders and foundations who recognized the good work of the land trust. This allowed for more staff expansion, including a two-person development team led by Development Director Jean Bowman, and a full-time land steward found in Grant Bronk, freeing up Jim Berkey to focus on the growing project load. In 2003, former director Greg Tollefson returned to the organization on a part-time basis to handle the Rock Creek work that had begun with Ellen Knight. The board, too, took up the challenge, assisting with fundraising, holding strategic planning sessions, and guiding and supporting the growing staff.

Given the realities of providing adequate staff and resources to meet the demand from conservation-minded landowners and agencies seeking help with public acquisitions, Five Valleys required a growing, long-term funding stream. Ninteman approached artist Kendahl Jan Jubb about the possibility of creating a license plate design that Five Valleys could submit to the State of Montana specialty license plate program. Jubb generously agreed, and the beautiful "Preserve the Place" license plates were quickly in great demand, with each plate bringing a $20 contribution to the organization every year. Her generosity turned out to truly be one of those gifts that keep on giving.

"Preserve the Place" by artist Kendahl Jan Jubb, was commissioned by Five Valleys for use in creating the organization's Montana license plate. *–Image courtesy of Murphy-Jubb Fine Art.*

Five Valleys' annual spring banquet was gradually becoming an extremely successful fundraising event, growing annually in attendance and dollars raised. It had quickly outgrown the spaces available at the Elks Club, the Double Tree Hotel, and the Governor's Ballroom at the Florence Hotel. Attendance had surpassed 300 supporters, with more than 100 local businesses providing auction items and cash support. Banquet tickets regularly sold out in a matter of a few short days.

One of the most consistently successful fundraising activities at the banquet was the briefcase raffle. The raffle, introduced and conducted by Gary Wolfe over the first several years, involved the sale of $20 tickets for a chance to walk away with a suitcase holding $1,000 in cash. The tickets sold in a matter of minutes, providing a nice $1,000 for the winner and a fine return for the cause. Quite often, the cash was either donated back or spent on another auction item.

In 1999 a most unique venue was secured–the lobby of Missoula International Airport. The lobby was filled with more than 320 supporters who contributed a total of $23,000 during the banquet. As visitor numbers to Missoula increased, it became impractical to host banquets at the airport, so the venue changed again, but it didn't move very far.

For the 2002 banquet, Northstar Aviation made their hangar available, and supporters gathered among the collection of classic and modern aircraft stored there. The thirtieth anniversary gathering in 2002 brought in $52,000.

For the 2003 banquet, the Northstar Aviation hangar was transformed. Decorations included a virtual forest of potted trees on loan from Caras Nursery adding a natural touch. Jim Valeo's vintage biplane was wheeled into the hangar for all to see, and later bid on for rides over the Five Great Valleys with Jim at the controls. The 2003 banquet also served as the unveiling and auction sale of the original Kendahl Jan Jubb painting that was used for the Five Valleys license plates. Nearly 400 friends of Five Valleys joined in the celebration, with new Missoula Mayor John Engen serving as master of ceremonies.

The 2002 thirtieth anniversary banquet in the Northstar Aviation hangar. *–Five Valleys Land Trust collections.*

The Alberton Gorge. *–Photo by Peter Dayton, Five Valleys Land Trust collections.*

EIGHT

LET'S BUY THE ALBERTON GORGE!

FORTY MILES WEST OF MISSOULA along the Clark Fork River in Mineral County lies the Alberton Gorge, one of western Montana's priceless natural treasures, as wild and beautiful today as it was when it was carved by the cataclysmic floods draining Glacial Lake Missoula 10,000 years ago.

By the 1990s, more than 30,000 adventurers were finding their way every summer to the sheer-walled canyon to challenge its daunting rapids in rafts and kayaks. Others sought the solitude and beauty of the shadowy canyon on foot. And still others knew that native cutthroat and bull trout lurked in the deep pools and eddies of the gorge.

Not simply a recreational treasure, the timbered slopes and remote location of the deep canyon offer habitat for many wildlife species. Its purple cliffs harbor falcon aeries. And it guards a vital undeveloped link for wildlife to move back and forth from the Northern Continental Divide ecosystem to the vast wild lands of the Selway-Bitterroot and beyond.

Marvelous as the Alberton Gorge is, the protection and public ownership of this unique landscape became a story unto itself.

In 2004, Five Valleys played a key role in assuring the protection of the Gorge forever. That's when Five Valleys completed the public acquisition of 8 miles of the Clark Fork River corridor, the culmination of a fifteen-year effort by a consortium of state and federal agencies, conservation groups, and whitewater enthusiasts.

Montana Power Company had acquired land along the Alberton Gorge between Alberton and Tarkio many decades ago, with an eye toward a possible dam site for future power generation. When that plan was abandoned as impracticable, the lands became surplus for the company, and they had indicated a willingness to work with state agencies and conservation groups to sell the property for eventual transfer into public ownership.

The effort to protect the Gorge began in the early 1990s when local whitewater enthusiasts, state and federal agencies, and the Montana Power Company first approached Five Valleys to explore ways to protect the canyon from residential development. The ultimate goal was to move the land into public ownership with Montana FWP. Montana Power Company engaged Bruce Bugbee to coordinate the effort. The collaboration, including Five Valleys, worked with Bugbee to find a path forward. When River Network, a national conservation organization, showed interest in the project, Five Valleys stepped back and River Network took the lead, entering into an option agreement with Montana Power Company in 1998 to purchase the company's lands in the Gorge.

Some conservation projects are short and straightforward. However, the Alberton Gorge was not to be one of those. Over the years, Bugbee had developed a reputation for his ability to fashion truly creative land protection transactions. The Alberton Gorge project may have been his most creative. It was certainly one of those efforts that might euphemistically be termed "elegant."

The plan devised by Bugbee, Montana Power, state and federal agencies, and conservation groups involved numerous interagency parcel swaps, outright sale of certain public property, and transfer of some public property to conservation interests for public sale to offset the purchase price payable to Montana Power for the Gorge property. Still seem simple?

Well, no.

As negotiations progressed and timelines changed, so did the players. In the early 2000s, Montana Power Company moved toward deregulation and reorganization, and its operations in western Montana were sold to NorthWestern Energy. In 2003, River Network announced that due to organizational restructuring it could not continue with the project. Five Valleys was asked to assume the lead role.

Five Valleys agreed to step in, and Tollefson assumed full-time Gorge project management duties for the land trust and a new title, special projects director. Peter Dayton, a whitewater enthusiast, local attorney with Worden Thane PC, and frequent advisor to Five Valleys, agreed to provide the necessary legal work pro-bono on what turned out to be an extremely complex transaction. In the ensuing twelve months, Tollefson worked to secure the necessary funding to acquire the NorthWestern Energy lands, while also working out details of a multi-part land exchange that made it possible.

How complex? Here's a small sampling of the details involved:

- Five Valleys needed to secure a $750,000 line of credit to assure adequate funding would be available at closing.
- A total of seventy separate parcels located in fifteen Montana counties were swapped among the USFS, Montana FWP, Montana Department of Natural Resources and Conservation, and NorthWestern Energy.
- Properties that changed hands included the former Montana FWP headquarters in Billings and the historic buildings and residential quarters at the base of Hebgen Dam, near West Yellowstone.
- Ten federal, state, and county agencies as well as the Montana State Land Board were involved.
- The transactions required full National Environmental Policy Act and Montana Environmental Policy Act compliance, full Environmental Impact Statement preparation, and public participation at all stages.
- The original purchase option had to be extended more than ten times to accommodate a multitude of delays.

The project required one more serious leap of faith for the Five Valleys Board of Directors to agree to move forward, but once they did, board members and supporters pitched in. Gary Wolfe, former president of the Rocky Mountain Elk Foundation and now a Five Valleys Board member, provided numerous whitewater tours of the Gorge to supporters and especially to potential donors. As the project timeline spooled out, so did the need to fundraise to keep it going. As a veteran of complicated conservation land transactions in his professional life, Wolfe urged Tollefson to provide some sort of visual schematic description of the project. Through trial and error, Tollefson finally came up with a graphic that, he claimed, illustrated literally and figuratively the complexity of the endeavor.

The Five Valleys community rallied, and fundraising help again came from far and wide. The effort included another beautiful watercolor creation by artist

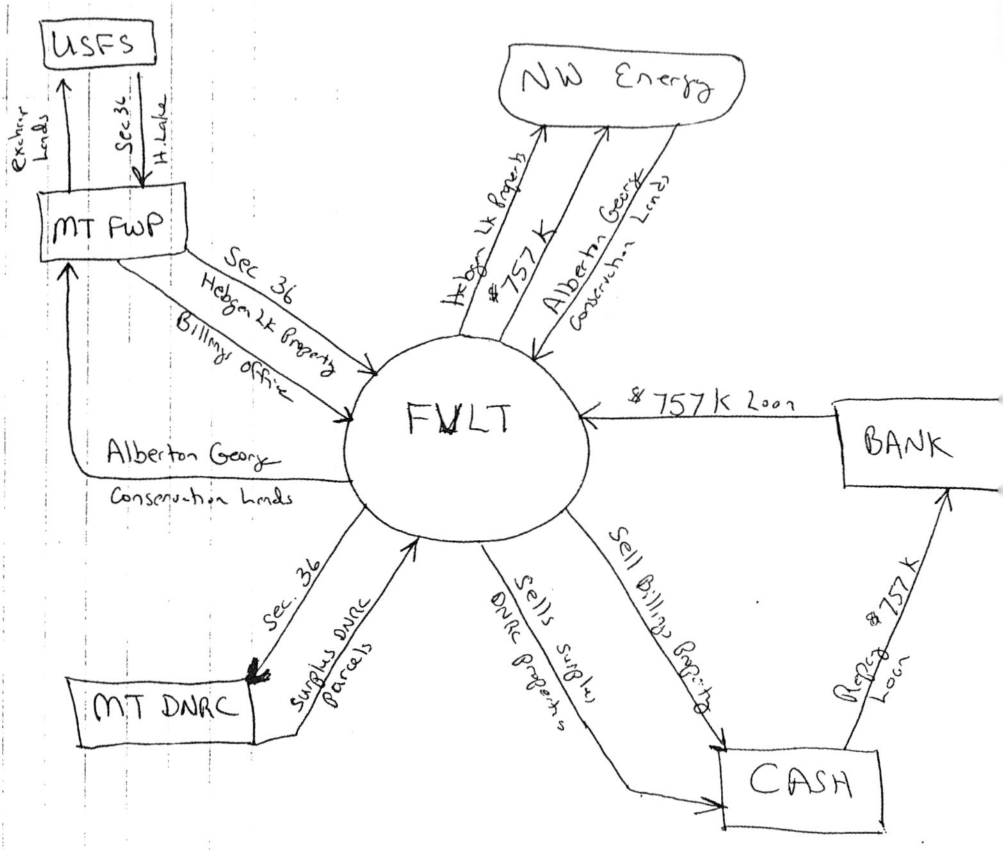

Greg Tollefson's sketch of the complex funding, acquisition, and land transfer process required to protect the Alberton Gorge between 2004 and 2014. *–Five Valleys Land Trust collections.*

Kendahl Jan Jubb. "Clark Fork Canyon" depicts one of the famed Ninemile wolves that range just north of the Gorge. Limited edition prints were sold to help increase awareness and raise funds for the project.

On November 30, 2004, the acquisition was finally completed, and the Gorge lands were transferred to public ownership with Montana FWP. However, Five Valleys did not have the luxury of celebrating for long.

As part of the exchange, Five Valleys acquired environmentally sensitive land near Tarkio and agreed to enter into a second land exchange with the Montana Department of Natural Resources and Conservation to protect the Tarkio lands and make certain "trade lands" further downstream available for private own-

"Clark Fork Canyon" by Kendahl Jan Jubb. *–Image courtesy of Murphy-Jubb Fine Art.*

ership. This allowed Mineral County to maintain its private land tax base while also providing an opportunity for Five Valleys to retire the debt incurred to purchase the Gorge. After the initial success and transfer to Montana FWP, it took until 2007 to complete the subsequent land exchanges. Final dispensation of the trade lands that Five Valleys acquired was not completed until 2014, over two decades after the project began.

The ultimate success of the Alberton Gorge project required collaborative relationships, goodwill, and long hours devoted to the project among Montana FWP, the USFS, Montana Department of Natural Resources and Conservation, Mineral County government, Five Valleys, and other groups. Once again, having the right people in the right place at the right time was the key. The right people included Lee Bastian, regional parks manager for Montana FWP; Kathy McAllister, deputy regional forester for the USFS's Northern Region; Bob Storer, trust lands manager for the Montana Department of Natural Resources and Conservation; and Judt Stang, Mineral County commissioner. Of course, Peter Dayton's monumental effort handling the legal aspects of this hugely complex transaction, along with Carol Billadeau of First American Title in Mineral County, were also nearly heroic. The success of those relationships led to several more public acquisitions in the lower Clark Fork area.

The Cedar Creek acquisition, another multi-year effort, involved the purchase of nearly 7 miles of riparian habitat along the stream, protecting critical habitat for native bull trout and westslope cutthroat. The land was made up of a collection of mining claims along the Cedar Creek, which flows into the Clark Fork River in the middle of the town of Superior. Bill Finnegan of Anaconda approached Five Valleys about assisting in moving the property into public ownership. His aunt, Grace Finnegan, who passed away at 91 in 2005, owned the property and had expressed her wish that it be sold for public use. Both the Lolo National Forest and Montana FWP had keen interest in the property because of its native fisheries value.

A colorful feature of this effort involved the negotiations to relocate a somewhat notorious, cantankerous character who had established residency on the property with permission of the landowner. Tollefson handled the negotiations; Chris Fagan, then a Five Valleys project manager, members of the Finnegan family, and Sander Tollefson, helped relocate the resident and removed the structures and improvements that had been constructed there. Five Valleys purchased the land, then transferred it to the USFS, and was reimbursed with funds from the Land and Water Conservation Fund, as well as other sources identified and secured by Montana FWP. Ladd Knotek, Montana FWP fisheries biologist for the lower Clark Fork area, and Brian Riggers, Lolo Forest fisheries biologist, were both key to securing most of the funding for the acquisition. The Cedar Creek transaction was completed in 2006.

Another enduring benefit of the Alberton Gorge project was the continuing relationship developed with Kathy McAllister, who, upon retirement from the Forest Service and after taking a short break, joined the Five Valleys Board and served for more than a decade, including a stint as board president. She continues to volunteer tirelessly, especially as member of the vital banquet committee.

The Cedar Creek parcel protected in 2006. –*Five Valleys Land Trust collections.*

McCauley Butte. *–Five Valleys Land Trust collections.*

NINE

THE WORKING LANDSCAPE AND A COMMITMENT TO THE FUTURE

ALTHOUGH FIVE VALLEYS' EXPANDING WORKING AREA now included the Alberton Gorge in Mineral County, as well as conservation easements in upper Rock Creek, the Blackfoot Valley, and the Upper Clark Fork, the organization continued to recognize and honor its commitment to the people and landscapes of Missoula County. From its earliest days, Five Valleys always had conservation easements in progress somewhere within view of the streets of Missoula.

That's why Five Valleys, at Ninteman's urging, took a lead role with the Missoula County Open Lands Advisory Committee in evaluating the feasibility of another open space bond. Funds from the 1995 bond, used to protect Mount Jumbo, Mount Sentinel, and so many other special places, were nearly exhausted. Ninteman hired recently returned Missoula native Donna Erickson, a landscape architect by training, to conduct research to understand the community's appetite for another bond. Upon discovering strong continued support for a robust open space program, and with the blessing of Missoula Mayor John Engen and the Missoula County commissioners, the group drafted bond language and a sophisticated campaign strategy worthy of the $10 million in bond funds that were being requested.

Pelah Hoyt, a native of the Jocko Valley north of Missoula and another UM environmental studies graduate, volunteered to help conduct listening and information sessions around Missoula County and generate support for the bond. Once again, Missoula voters flocked to the polls in 2006, just as they had done in 1995, to support protection of the precious open lands with an incredible 70% of the vote.

"I couldn't be more gratified, relieved and excited," Ninteman told *Missoulian* reporter Perry Backus the night of the election. "This vote shows a lot of foresight. People here really care about the landscape and are willing to find creative ways to protect it."

Once again, a volunteer with Five Valleys did such impressive work that they were hired as soon as feasible. Pelah Hoyt was brought on to help handle Five Valleys' continuously growing stewardship load and fairly quickly moved on to land protection. The learning curve for land trust work is steep, but Hoyt was soon handling easement projects from start to finish. She would stay on for the next seventeen years and create her own legacy of important conservation achievements with Five Valleys.

With the addition of Hoyt, Ninteman's staff now numbered nine strong. It included Hoyt, Berkey, Fagan, and Tollefson working in land protection and stewardship; Elizabeth Drummond as Banquet Coordinator; Glenn Marangelo as Development Director; and Meredith Printz as Office Manager.

This era also continued the long tradition of having community champions as board members. Between 2005-2008, Five Valleys Board members included Sean

Five Valleys staff, friends and family hike Mount Jumbo, April 2007. From left: Chris Fagan, Anna Fagan, Bill Drummond, Glenn Marangelo, Greg Tollefson, Wendy Ninteman, Pelah Hoyt, Elizabeth Drummond, Jim Berkey, and Meredith Printz. *–Five Valleys Land Trust collections.*

Benton, Laura Brehm, Ann Boone, Cooper Burchenal, Sandra Burner, Jim Cusker, Tom Demmons, Amy Duerk, Betty duPont, Charlie Eiseman, Julie Gardner, Jim Kenyon, Susan Masar, John Menson, Ciche Pitcher, Julia Riber, Jim Royan, John Scibek, Amber Sherrill, Don Sokoloski, John Talbot, Chuck Tribe, Rod Tripke, Jim Valeo, Bob Whaley, Nancy Winslow, and Gary Wolfe. Members duPont, Masar, and Whaley would all graciously exit by 2008, each having served the organization for a dozen years or more.

The year 2007 was a banner year for Missoula open space advocates. That year, two more cornerstone properties were protected with a series of conservation easements.

First came a donated easement that protected much of McCauley Butte, the promontory beyond Fort Missoula on the southwest corner of the community along the Bitterroot River. The easement not only protected the scenic qualities of the parcel, it also restricted new development to one residence on the 257-acre property and protected nearly 1 mile of rich riparian habitat and cottonwood gallery along the Bitterroot River.

Board members at a 2008 retreat. From left: Jim Royan, John Talbot, Amy Duerk, Will Ballew, Amber Sherrill, Ciche Pitcher, Sean Benton, John Menson, Chuck Tribe, Charlie Eiseman, Jim Brown, Jim Valeo, Nancy Winslow, and Jim Cusker. *–Five Valleys Land Trust collections.*

Next came a series of easements to protect the family ranchlands replete with beautiful open grassland, timbered slopes, and important wildlife habitat at the southeast corner of Missoula beneath Mount Dean Stone. Three families holding most of visible open lands above existing developments in the South Hills–the Line, Rimel, and Hayden families–approached Five Valleys about protecting their cherished family lands in perpetuity while also allowing and encouraging continued agricultural uses.

Ninteman spent many hours working with the families over several years to shape easements that reflected the landowners' conservation vision and Five Valleys' conservation priorities. The four easements, which all closed within two months of each other and protected a combined 1,000-plus acres, not only protect wildlife and aesthetic open space values, but also ensure the land will be available for agricultural use in the years ahead.

As is so often the case, the Lines, the Rimels, and the Haydens were strong supporters of the work of Five Valleys long before the easement discussions began, and their support for the organization has not faded since.

"We hope generations to come will benefit from us making a good decision today," landowner Chris Line told the *Missoulian* on October 16, 2007. "We all think this will be a good direction for our community."

John Rimel agreed, saying, "In the course of my life, this is the biggest decision that I've made since the day I asked my wife, Karen, to marry me. They've both been very good decisions."

As if echoing those sentiments with future action, John Rimel would become a valued Five Valleys Board member and the Line family would help Five Valleys achieve another major conservation goal in the years ahead.

Another 2007 easement, this one a 268-acre farm and ranchland easement with the Iverson family in the Potomac Valley, would yield still another future Five Valleys Board member. Denny Iverson, working with his mother, Doris, and brother, Les, would complete the first of two easements on their family ranch. Denny would also join the board, providing a valuable agricultural perspective, serve as Board President, and become an able champion for the protection of the working landscapes.

Despite the expansion of land protection staff, Ninteman managed to always have conservation easement projects to work on, in addition to increasing orga-

The Line, Rimel, and Hayden conservation easements in Missoula's South Hills. *–Photo by Kip Sikora, Five Valleys Land Trust collections.*

Denny Iverson (above) and Les Iverson on their ranch in the Potomac Valley. *–Photo by Nelson Kenter, Five Valleys Land Trust collections.*

nizational responsibilities. A majority of these easement projects focused on protection of the "working landscape," that is, lands under agricultural use. Some of Ninteman's signature easement projects include:

- The Sundance Ranch, totaling 750 acres of lush grasslands, riparian habitat, and timbered uplands in the North Fork of the Blackfoot near Ovando.
- Primm Meadow, 113 acres of magnificent old-growth ponderosa pine in the upper reaches of Gold Creek in the Blackfoot. Board member Marcia Hogan and USFS historian Libby Langston collaborated on a beautiful, award-winning film, *Pines of Primm Meadow*, to memorialize the event.
- The Louise Dean ranch, 160 acres of wetlands and grasslands just outside of Lincoln in the Upper Blackfoot.
- The Schroeder Ranch, 640 acres of timber, grasslands, and riparian habitat near the very headwaters of the Blackfoot River.
- The Spinetta easement, 144 acres straddling the West Fork of the Bitterroot above Painted Rocks Reservoir.
- The Harrison Ranch, 380 acres of scenic and productive agricultural land in the Potomac Valley.
- The Valeo Ranch, 362 acres of productive farmland along the Clark Fork River in the Grass Valley. Jim and Marci Valeo donated the easement, which is adjacent to the Cusker Ranch; Jim became a board member and later board president, and continues to work tirelessly in support of Five Valleys' efforts.

This era also saw the Five Valleys office emerge from the dungeon-like basement to a spacious office on the top floor of the First National Bank, just across Higgins Avenue, to accommodate expanding staff needs. For quite a while, the new experience with having windows served as a daily reminder of Five Valleys' good fortune.

A few years later, Five Valleys moved again to the suite above Office City at 115 West Broadway, this time with a series of offices that allowed for actual quiet workspaces. The move to West Broadway was memorable in many ways, not the least of which was the enthusiastic assistance of Missoula Mayor John Engen among the many volunteers hauling furniture and filing cabinets out of the old

Louise Dean and her dog, Hawk, on her upper Blackfoot Valley conservation easement property. *–Photo by Michael Gallacher, Five Valleys Land Trust collections.*

offices, down through the adjacent city parking garage, and around the corner to the new offices.

One of the most spectacular moments in the move came when board member Jim Valeo loaded his pickup and started down through the parking garage with desks, chairs, and bookcases stacked high. Stacked too high, as it turned out. Those who were standing there and saw it coming were awestruck as bookcases and chairs cracked and splintered spectacularly, falling to the concrete floor like flotsam and jetsam. Since most of the damaged goods were already hand-me-downs, replacing a few bookcases and chairs was not a major setback. That move completed, Five Valleys was not yet done with its nomadic office life. There were a couple more office locations still to come.

UNDER NINTEMAN'S LEADERSHIP, Five Valleys also took a lead role in developing a statewide organization of Montana land trusts in 2005. The Montana Association of Land Trusts (MALT) works with the Montana Legislature, other government agencies, the Land Trust Alliance, and other groups to encourage legislation that enables land trusts to continue to work effectively. MALT also keeps an eagle eye out to discourage legislation that might undermine the work of land trusts. With twelve land trust members, MALT is a respected organization on the Montana political scene and with Congress.

Looking at landscape-level conservation regionally, Ninteman was also among the leaders of an effort to bring together land trusts in the Northern Rocky Mountains under an umbrella group known as the Heart of the Rockies Initiative. The group seeks to share scarce resources, plan strategically on a much more ambitious level, and work together for the broader interests of conservation. Paul Sihler, former deputy director of Montana FWP, was hired as inaugural director of the new organization, with Five Valleys serving as fiscal sponsor. The Heart of the Rockies Initiative is now a fully stand-alone organization, consisting of land

Ancient Ponderosa Pine trees on the Primm Meadow conservation easement property.
–Photo by Lena Viall, Five Valleys Land Trust collections.

trusts and other land conservation organizations from five states and two Canadian provinces.

On the national scene, Five Valleys became the first land trust in Montana, and among the first land trusts in the country, to achieve full accreditation by participating in the Land Trust Alliance's new accreditation pilot program. To do so, the organization worked with Donna Erickson to codify a set of policies and procedures that guaranteed it was in complete compliance with the standards and practices established by the Land Trust Alliance.

As 2007 came to a close, Ninteman stepped aside as executive director to assume new challenges as the Western Director of the Land Trust Alliance. After a nationwide search, Five Valleys' new executive director was found close to home. Grant Kier, a former consulting geologist, and more recently the executive director of the Bitter Root Land Trust, was hired for the post.

Wendy Ninteman had led Five Valleys to the cusp of a significant milestone, over 40,000 acres of land protected with 101 conservation easements and a number of major public acquisitions. Conservation easements were in place in all of the Five Great Valleys. The staff had increased from three to a talented professional group of nine. And, most noteworthy, Five Valleys had become one of the recognized leaders among regional land trusts in the entire country.

The Moiese Valley Ranch conservation easement property near Charlo. *–Photo by Cathrine L. Walters, Five Valleys Land Trust collections.*

TEN

BUILDING ON SUCCESS AND THE CHALLENGE OF PERPETUITY

GRANT KIER DID NOT HAVE TO REINVENT THE WHEEL when he assumed the directorship of the organization. The transition was smooth, and many projects were moving through the Five Valleys pipeline, including a mix of private conservation easements and public acquisitions. Kier brought new energy and a vision for future growth, expanded partnerships, and quickly launched a new strategic planning process to update conservation priorities throughout the now nine county working area.

It wasn't long before the organization once again outgrew its workspace and would take over two floors of offices in the 200 block of West Front Street. Meanwhile, some of the faces were changing at Five Valleys. Jim Berkey, who had been with the organization from the early days, moved on to The Nature Conservancy as a program manager for southwest Montana. Kier asked Greg Tollefson to stay on as conservation director. And a vacancy in the stewardship staff also had to be filled.

Another volunteer who happened to be in the right place at the right time got the nod for the stewardship job. Ryan Chapin had secured his first job in Montana by jumping a fence and flagging down a rancher doing some irrigation work. He got a job on the spot. When he joined the Five Valleys team in 2008, he brought that kind of drive and willingness to tackle the most gnarly tasks. Chris Fagan, who had put his law career on hold for several years as a Five Valleys project manager, decided it was time to move back into law. Juniper Davis soon joined the staff as an attorney and project manager after recently returning to her hometown, eager to follow in her grandfather John Talbot's footsteps at Five Valleys. Alina Niklison

McCue, a biologist and passionate conservationist, signed on as a part-time land steward and multi-purpose staffer. With all the enthusiastic new blood, Five Valleys was an exciting place for all to work.

And there was plenty of work to do. The 2010 census found the population of Missoula County to be almost 110,000, a jump of another 15,000 newcomers from 2000. That kind of growth demands response from those interested in maintaining the quality of life so long enjoyed by local residents. Although growth in outlying counties in the Five Valleys working area may not have been quite so dramatic, the need to protect what was left, and to provide public access where possible, continued to grow as well. On December 1, 2010, Finnegan's Family Restaurant, proudly spanning Rattlesnake Creek for so many years, closed its doors. Employees were given no advance notice. No meatloaf this year.

The theme over the tenure of Kier's work at Five Valleys may be best encapsulated with the phrase "connecting people to places." A new emphasis on working with community members around western Montana to respond to specific needs, sometimes in unexpected ways, became a guide for Five Valleys' conservation work.

The Sunny Slope Grazing Association conservation easement property. –*Five Valleys Land Trust collections.*

To wit: In the spring of 2008, the Sunny Slope Grazing Association and Five Valleys, with support from The Nature Conservancy, Montana FWP, the US Fish and Wildlife Service, the Big Blackfoot Chapter of Trout Unlimited, and the Blackfoot Challenge, completed a landmark conservation easement project. The Sunny Slope Grazing Association conservation easement protected 7,570 acres in the Blackfoot Valley, the largest in Five Valleys' history to that point. It was the first Montana easement project directly aimed at protecting fisheries habitat, conserving more than 14 miles of spawning tributaries for native westslope cutthroat and bull trout.

Later that year, Five Valleys facilitated the eventual establishment of a Montana FWP river access site at Bearmouth on the Upper Clark Fork River by accepting a gift of land along the river from rancher Gene Tripp. Five Valleys would hold the parcel for several years while Montana FWP completed the necessary administrative steps required to take title and assume management.

In Mineral County, Five Valleys facilitated the Forest Service's purchase of 15 miles of the defunct Milwaukee Railroad right-of-way for use as recreational trail along the Route of the Olympian that would connect with the popular Route of the Hiawatha Trail into Idaho. Five Valleys secured options to purchase ten privately held parcels, closing on those purchases in 2009 and transferring them to the management of the USFS a few months later. This work would be complemented in 2013 when Five Valleys transferred another portion of the trail, including the historic trestle at Saltese, to the USFS. Due to some copyright considerations, this portion of the continuous trail was named after another of the Milwaukee Railroad's popular passenger trains, the Olympian; hence, the Route of the Olympian.

A few other examples of this broadened vision include:

- Enabling the expansion of, and increased access to, Milltown State Park. Five Valleys acquired, then transferred, key lands on the western and southwestern edge of the park, including the overlook site off Deer Creek Road and the trailhead located there, to Montana FWP.
- Protecting private working lands in the picturesque Woodworth Meadows area near Seeley Lake by working with landowners to develop a conservation plan and protect the private lands within the vital wildlife corridor. Five Valleys now holds conservation easements covering nearly 500 acres of that meadow.

The Saltese trestle along the Route of the Olympian Trail. *–Five Valleys Land Trust collections.*

- Conserving a swath of Missoula's North Hills through a unique partnership with solid waste corporate giant, Allied Waste. Allied Waste donated a conservation easement on more than 300 acres of land immediately adjacent to the existing Missoula landfill. The easement limits future expansion of the landfill, protecting a large portion of the North Hills and buffering lands that were earlier protected by easement or acquired by the City of Missoula as part of the Rattlesnake Greenway. The area holds special importance for the substantial elk herd that winters on the property. Now owned by Republic Services, the land will also be the eventual location of a pedestrian trail that will expand public access across the entire North Hills.
- Placing a conservation easement across nearly 2,300 acres of the Moiese Valley Ranch, a working ranch and dairy in the Mission Valley that tied together thousands of acres of public and tribal lands. Highly visible from the Ninepipe National Wildlife Refuge and the Confederated Salish and

Kootenai Tribes' Bison Range, the easement also protected the hillside that boasts the "C" for the town of Charlo.

In 2010, Five Valleys would complete a milestone project. The 3,774-acre Peterson Angus Ranch overlooks Drummond and the Flint Creek Valley. The ranch holds some of the region's most pristine montane grasslands, carefully tended by its conservation-minded landowners, Sue and Randy Peterson, who granted a conservation easement on their family ranch. As a part of Montana Natural Resource Damage Claim Program funding requirements, the project established a pedestrian trail on the ranch that gives visitors a chance to hike to the top of Beacon Hill. From this vantage point, the Bearmouth area of the Garnet Range is in clear view, as is the entirety of the Flint Creek Range, the John Long Mountains, the Sapphire Range, the Clark Fork Valley toward Garrison Junction, and the peaks of Pintlar Range to the south. The project launched the conservation momentum that would build in the Flint Creek and Upper Clark Fork Valleys through the following decade and beyond.

Stewardship activities across Five Valleys' working area expanded significantly during this time. In addition to the very serious responsibility of monitoring compliance on all easements held by Five Valleys, staff worked with landowners

Randy and Sue Peterson on their conservation easement property near Drummond. *–Photo by Grant Kier, Five Valleys Land Trust collections.*

The 2012 Five Valleys staff. From left: Jillian Shepard Seaton, Holly Biehl, Sarah Richey, Maggie Pittman, Beth Cosgswell, Lewis Kogan, Glenn Marangelo, Grant Kier, Ryan Chapin, Pelah Hoyt, and Jenny Tollefson. *–Photo by Nancy de Pastino, Five Valleys Land Trust collections.*

to solve a variety of day-to-day challenges such as weed management, grazing issues, habitat enhancement, riparian fencing, and more. Jenny Tollefson, who had been completing baseline easement reports on a contract basis, came on full-time to fill a role as stewardship coordinator.

By 2012, Five Valleys' staff had reached ten full- or part-time employees, and everyone had more than a full portfolio of projects or responsibilities. In addition to the projects already mentioned, two particularly challenging and perhaps visionary efforts were launched during this period. First, however, a little housekeeping was in order.

With Five Valleys' now substantial staff, an ever-growing project load, and a large number of conservation easements requiring perpetual stewardship, office space was at a premium. Kim and Ruth Reineking, longtime Five Valleys supporters and conservationists, came forward with a generous proposal.

The Reinekings were intimately familiar with the work of Five Valleys. They had been engaged with both Five Valleys and the Rock Creek Trust for years, and also supported the work of Montana Trout Unlimited and the Westslope Chapter of Trout Unlimited. Ruth had served as president of that organization, and Kim had served on the Rock Creek Advisory Council and as a member of the Five

Valleys Board of Directors. The Reinekings had also donated a conservation easement to Five Valleys, perpetually protecting their property on Rock Creek.

An old railroad warehouse on Hickory Street, near McCormick Park and adjacent to the Kim Williams River Trail, had been acquired by the Montana Natural History Center for its new offices back in 2005. The building had previously been the site of Big Sky Brewing Company's first headquarters. More recently, the Montana Natural History Center was renting out the east end of the building while planning a remodel of the west end where their offices were established. When the tenants left, it provided an opportunity for the Reinekings to purchase that portion of the building from Montana Natural History Center, with the idea of creating a new home for Five Valleys. Because the two organizations shared complementary missions, overlapping memberships and supporters, and also recognized potential for a variety of collaborative efforts in the future, it seemed like a perfect match.

Reineking Construction completely rebuilt the east half of the building for Five Valleys. The Reinekings then offered to lease the beautiful new building to Five Valleys with a unique twenty-year lease-to-own agreement.

The new building included private office spaces, large and small meeting rooms, a spacious reception area, and plenty of administrative and storage space, thanks to the generosity and vision of the Reinekings. Beautiful in design, the office was constructed with cutting-edge energy efficiency in mind. In a nod to the many artists and photographers whose work has helped bring projects to life in the mind of the public, the freshly painted walls were adorned with dozens of works of art. Many of the pieces were donated by supporters, board members, or the local artists and photographers themselves. It is a welcoming and worthy place to do the work of conservation.

Ruth and Kim Reineking. *–Photo courtesy of Ruth and Kim Reineking.*

Five Valleys Land Trust's office at 120 Hickory Street. *–Five Valleys Land Trust collections.*

With all the new elbow room, Five Valleys had a lot to celebrate at the 2012 annual banquet, including the fortieth anniversary of the organization. By this time, the venue had again changed. The event packed the UM University Center Ballroom and raised over $140,000 from 460 attendees. Twenty local businesses pitched in as sponsors, including First Interstate Bank, the successor to First National Bank, who had partnered with FVRPA on the Jacobs Island project forty years prior. Combined with 140 silent and live auction donors, the 2012 banquet was a rousing success.

The success of the annual banquets is, of course, not without its challenges. But over the period beginning about 2010 on through the next decade, a relentless banquet committee spent months planning and organizing those banquets, down to the smallest detail. Longtime board members Pam Volkmann, Mary Lynn Eiseman, Kathy McAllister, Jim Cusker, Jim Valeo, and former board member Mae Nan Ellingson, as well community volunteers and past staff including Elizabeth Drummond, put in a tremendous amount of work every year to assure the success of the event.

Kathy McAllister and Pam Volkmann. –*Photo by Tom Robertson, Five Valleys Land Trust collections.*

The 2012 Five Valleys' banquet in the University of Montana's University Center Ballroom. *–Photo by John Belobraidic, Five Valleys Land Trust collections.*

SOON THEREAFTER, FIVE VALLEYS ACCEPTED THE STEWARDSHIP RESPONSIBILITIES OF THE RATTLESNAKE LAND TRUST, an organization that had grown out of Save Open Space, the group that played a role in the 1995 open space bond and the protection of Mount Jumbo. The Rattlesnake Land Trust had accepted six conservation easements in the Missoula Valley that protected nearly 200 acres, including portions of Mount Jumbo and the North Hills, the Peschel conservation easement that includes a section of the popular public trail on Waterworks Hill, and the historic McKinnon-Flynn Ranch.

In 2011, the all-volunteer Rattlesnake Land Trust began conversations with Five Valleys about transferring their easement portfolio to Five Valleys, which had capacity to handle the perpetual obligations of easement stewardship. The transfer was finalized in late 2014.

"It was a big task to meet the challenge of perpetuity," Kier was quoted as saying in the December 22, 2014, *Missoulian*. "They were looking for someone to carry on their tradition, and we were happy to do it."

The Peschel family conservation easement in Missoula's North Hills. *–Photo by Jahrig Media.*

ELEVEN

COMMUNITY CONSERVATION

WAY BACK IN THE EARLY DAYS, the Rock Creek Trust hired Bruce Bugbee's planning group to identify important conservation lands held privately in the Rock Creek watershed. Bugbee's group identified and ranked these important private lands in order of conservation priority. One of the most highly rated parcels in lower Rock Creek was a 200-acre ranch at the confluence of Rock Creek and the Clark Fork River.

The parcel, formerly the Corra Ranch, created a welcome visual gateway to the precious Rock Creek Valley. The property also held significant value as wildlife habitat and a wildlife travel corridor. Efforts to craft a conservation outcome for the property had gone on without success for many years with several different landowners.

When a developer appeared on the scene with plans for a high-density residential development including construction of a 9-acre pond near the blue-ribbon waters of Rock Creek, nearby residents and the general public voiced strong objections. A lively and often rancorous debate raged on for some time. Of particular concern to a local group, the Rock Creek Protective Association, and to such organizations as Montana Trout Unlimited and the Clark Fork Coalition, was the potential for groundwater and surface water pollution and the danger posed to Rock Creek's prized wild trout fishery through the existence of a pond that could invite a variety of introduced species.

Despite these strong and valid concerns, the developer had already constructed the pond at dimensions that exceeded the approved size. A 10-foot-high gravel berm had been constructed to block any view of the property by travelers on Rock Creek Road. The subdivision process was closing in on final approval, but

The Rock Creek Confluence property as seen here in 2011 when it was slated for subdivision and included an ornamental pond. *Five Valleys Land Trust collections.*

public resistance continued to grow. Yard signs and billboards appeared up and down the creek, demanding, "No subdivision in Rock Creek!" The dispute was on the verge of turning very ugly.

A standard policy for land trusts is the avoidance of adversarial land use situations. A land trust, however, can enter the picture if an avenue is available that provides a solution to the dispute.

The great recession of 2008 took a heavy toll on construction and development as the bottom fell out of the housing market. In 2012, through the persistence of Kier to find a solution, Five Valleys negotiated a purchase agreement with the developer. Once again, Five Valleys set out to create a partnership capable of completing the purchase, but this time with the added challenge of restoring the ranch to its pre-development state. Because the property encompassed the confluence of Rock Creek and the Clark Fork River, it became known as the Confluence Project, known around Five Valleys simply as the Confluence.

With the help of funds from the 2006 Missoula County open space bond, the Montana Natural Resource Damage Claim Program, Montana Trout Unlimited, the

Westslope Chapter Trout Unlimited, the Montana Fish and Wildlife Conservation Trust, the Clark Fork Coalition, the Rock Creek Protective Association, and the generosity of neighboring landowners, particularly Ron Clausen, John and Sharene Menson, and Roy O'Connor, and lovers of Rock Creek in general, the purchase of two parcels, one on each side of Rock Creek Road, was completed in 2012.

That may make it sound too easy. Putting the 294-acre deal together was a complicated and challenging process. Rock Creek, however, is a special place among special places in western Montana. The intricate details of the several transactions involved and the different requirements from various funding sources made things tricky. But the deal was done.

What was different about the Confluence, however, was that Five Valleys didn't have a clear game plan for transferring the property to a public entity. It was a giant leap for the board and the organization to accept such a large and open-ended responsibility.

"We're wondering if there is a new model of public-private partnership to manage land for public benefit," Kier told reporter Rob Chaney for the December

Executive Director Grant Kier, Rock Creek landowner and Rock Creek Advisory Council member Roy O'Connor, and Montana Governor Steve Bullock lead a crowd touring the newly purchased Rock Creek Confluence property in July 2015. *–Photo by Tom Robertson, Five Valleys Land Trust collections.*

21, 2012, *Missoulian*. "I expect we'll spend a few years exploring that," Kier said. "But for the foreseeable future, we're owning this."

The significance of the project was highlighted in July 2015, when Governor Steve Bullock toured the Confluence as a part of "Montana Open Land Month."

"Montana open lands are a promise to future generations–our children and grandchildren–that the state that we call home, the state that we love, will be protected for them, so that rather than hearing from us about all of the amazing things that Montana once was, they can experience these things firsthand," Bullock said.

It comes with all acquisition projects. When the funds have been exchanged and the deeds delivered, whoever has ultimately taken ownership of a precious piece of real estate faces the realization of their obligation to care for the acquired land. When the buyer is a conservation group, taking care of the land may require adhering to higher standards than it would otherwise.

Restoration work began at once, with Five Valleys staff, chiefly Ryan Chapin and Jenny Tollefson, planning and implementing removal of the berm, weed eradication, restoration of native vegetation, and trail and access development. There

Clinton School students and educators help with restoration of the Confluence's former pond site through Clark Fork Coalition's Riparian Rx program, spring 2017; Five Valleys stewardship Director Jenny Tollefson and longtime volunteer Steve German at far right. *–Photo courtesy of Clark Fork Coalition.*

were fences to be removed and fences to build, and public access locations to be carefully planned and constructed. Irrigation water rights were relinquished, the flow now remaining in Rock Creek. The ranch house needed serious repairs. And, of course, there were many day-to-day concerns that would arise.

But this was Rock Creek, after all. Hundreds of individuals, landowners, volunteers and many organizations continue to help with the project, which now, a decade later, has become a living, evolving classroom. For all its challenges, or perhaps because of them, the Confluence proved to be a place where community, partnerships, and innovation thrived.

Early on, students from the Missoula College's Heavy Equipment Operation Program were enlisted to help remove the berm and recontour the ornamental pond into a wetland naturally fed by the ebbs and flows of Rock Creek, getting hands-on experience in the process. Following suit, graduate students from UM and seventh-graders from Clinton School developed and carried out land restoration prescriptions for the pond site, which saw hundreds of shrubs and saplings, and many pounds of native plant seed mix, planted by both students and volunteers. Veterans' groups helped thin neglected stands of timber. Hands on the Land volunteers came out annually to pull weeds. A bird banding station run by university researchers set up shop on the eastern Confluence parcel by the river. Elders from the Séliš-Ql̓ispé Culture Committee of the Confederated Salish and Kootenai Tribes made a pilgrimage to the Confluence, marking the first time tribal members could enjoy legal access to this important site in generations. The work kept staff busy commuting the 26 miles between Missoula and Rock Creek.

While protecting and restoring the land were top on the to-do list, public access development would come to be the true innovation of Five Valleys' work at the Confluence. In 2017, Rex Koenig approached Five Valleys about completing his Eagle Scout project on the property. With the blessing and oversight of staff, the Boy Scouts dug a 1/3-mile trail from Rock Creek Road to the former pond site–now a regenerating wetland–with the aim of making the trail a route suitable for people of all abilities.

Learning that the new trail proved quite challenging for those using wheelchairs, Five Valleys brought on UM Recreation Management student Brenden Dalin to improve the trail. Dalin's education and personal experience provided an invaluable resource.

With guidance from Summit Independent Living, a local disability advocacy nonprofit, the trail was much improved and has continued to be improved since. Summit Independent Living and Dalin have continued to be invaluable partners of Five Valleys' ongoing public access work, helping ensure that trails and interpretation are truly accessible at the Confluence and beyond.

Brenden Dalin and a Montana Conservation Corps member help design the Confluence's universal trail in 2018. *–Photo by Olga Helmy. Five Valley Land Trust collections.*

The success and momentum of the Confluence project led Five Valleys to engage in three other community open space efforts that would have a tremendous impact on the role Five Valleys would play in the years to come.

In 2015, the organization agreed to take title and assume management of 160 acres of former industrial timberland on Marshall Mountain, the once beloved ski area above the West Riverside neighborhood east of Missoula. Many Missoulians had grown up getting their first taste of powder on Marshall. But by the early 2000s, the ski area was shuttered due to increasingly unreliable snowfall. The middle portion of the mountain, above the ski area base, had previously been acquired by The Nature Conservancy as part of their Montana Legacy Project, and The Nature Conservancy now transferred that portion to Five Valleys. A community celebration was held in July 2015 to commemorate this transfer, complete with speeches, a bouncy house, food trucks, beer donated by Big Sky Brewing Company, and a ceremony to honor longtime Missoula Mayor John

Amber Sherrill, Missoula Mayor John Engen, The Nature Conservancy in Montana Executive Director Richard Jeo, and Grant Kier at Marshall Mountain, 2015. *–Tom Robertson Photography, Five Valleys Land Trust collections.*

Mountain bikers at Marshall Mountain. *–Photo by Tom Robertson, Five Valleys Land Trust collections.*

Engen for his ardent support of conservation and The Nature Conservancy for their leadership and partnership.

As with many parcels acquired over the years, Five Valleys intended to transfer its portion of Marshall Mountain to a public agency. But, now having the positive and educational experience of land management at the Confluence, Five Valleys chose to look at community needs for inspiration. Enter a partnership with a new non-profit, Mountain Bike Missoula.

Led by executive director Ben Horan and trails director Brian Williams, and with significant support from Big Sky Brewing Company and a host of eager volunteers, Mountain Bike Missoula would construct over 6 miles of world-class mountain biking trails across Five Valleys' portion of Marshall. These new trails helped reduce pressure on neighboring open lands and offered a place where schoolchildren, biking enthusiasts, and competitive riders alike could hone and showcase their skills.

Around that same time, Five Valleys became engaged in discussions about creating a public river park near Lincoln. The Blackfoot River cuts through the small, unincorporated town that lies nestled amid the Helena-Lewis and Clark National Forest. As Lincoln grew, new neighbors shunned the laissez faire-style access once enjoyed by locals. By the new millennium, the only public access point for residents to visit their hometown river was 4 miles from town.

Paul Roos at the Lincoln Community River Park, 2016. –*Five Valleys Land Trust collections.*

Partnering with legendary fishing guide, conservationist and Lincoln native Paul Roos, Five Valleys entered into a purchase agreement for Roos's 9-acre parcel on the south bank of the Blackfoot, just a half mile from Lincoln's only stoplight. Using Lewis and Clark County Land, Water, and Wildlife bond funds and partnering with the Helena-based Prickly Pear Land Trust, Five Valleys purchased the Lincoln Community River Park parcel from Roos in late 2016. Now a popular and thriving river park, Five Valleys owns and manages the site in concert with the residents of Lincoln. One cannot help but draw connections between this river park and FVRPA's first project at Jacobs Island four decades before.

Waiting in the wings was another community open space project. It was to be an effort that enjoyed a number of stages worthy of victory celebrations on their own. The new project, however, had the habit of expanding the vision and determination of the organization as each new stage was completed.

Lander Schwab, son of Executive Director Whitney Schwab, enjoys the Lincoln Community River Park, 2017. *–Photo by Whitney Schwab, Five Valleys Land Trust collections.*

Mount Dean Stone, as seen from the North Hills, with the South Hills Spur illuminated by sunlight. *–Photo by Grant Kier, Five Valleys Land Trust collections.*

TWELVE

ANOTHER CORNERSTONE CHALLENGE

THERE IS AN OBVIOUS AND PROMINENT BARE KNOLL on the shoulder of Mount Dean Stone, above the mouth of Pattee Canyon. Much of the face of the mountain on the west side, above the residential developments on the South Hills, had been protected with conservation easements in 2007. From the knoll, visitors can take in the rolling, open south face of Mount Sentinel, and on toward Mount Jumbo, the North Hills, and the Rattlesnake Valley. To the east lies Pattee Canyon, from bottom to top. Below and to the west, the growing city of Missoula seems to stretch all the way to Frenchtown. Blue Mountain rises to the southwest on USFS land, scarred by the last big fires. In the distance, the peaks of the Ninemile Divide and the Great Burn Wilderness Study Area along the Bitterroot divide shine in the sunlight.

The knoll had long been a conservation priority for Five Valleys. Wendy Ninteman had begun discussions with the landowners in the early 2000s but was never able to come to acceptable terms. Then, within the span of two serendipitous weeks in 2014, two calls came in.

The landowner of the knoll, Davis Clapp, was now interested in divesting himself of the property. Clapp and lands director Hoyt went back and forth in negotiations for months, dragging into the next year. Kier, wanting to show the board the potential of the project, arranged for a spring 2015 board meeting to be held on the knoll. That morning, as Hoyt was driving up to present about the project to the board, who were seated in a ring of chairs in the grass, she pulled her truck over to take a phone call. There, on the side of the road, Hoyt and Clapp came to an agreement.

Later that year, with help from private donors and Five Valleys special protection funds, the purchase of the 83-acre knoll that had become known as the South Hills Spur was completed.

With that acquisition, another challenging conservation project blossomed and grew into a long-term vision that would eventually provide public access from the South Hills Spur all the way to Miller Creek, linking with Pattee Canyon trails and public open spaces both to the south and north. It was another of the very complicated projects involving multiple private owners, multiple partners, and huge funding challenges.

Recognizing the potential to build on the Spur purchase to develop public access to the summit of Dean Stone and beyond, Kier engaged in discussions with The Nature Conservancy, which owned 2,500 acres above Miller Creek on the south side of the mountain. The Nature Conservancy had acquired the land from Plum Creek Timber Company as part of the Montana Legacy Project and was searching for a conservation-minded buyer and outcome for the land. Kier made the public announcement of this new opportunity at the 2016 banquet, a surprise that seemed to fill the UM Ballroom with excitement and stoke the bidding at the annual event.

An auction item called "Fund a Dream" had become a regular part of the annual banquet, asking supporters to hold up their auction number in response to funding a certain project at certain levels, beginning with high sums, and descending until everyone in attendance so inclined can participate.

That evening's 500 generous attendees pledged $215,000 to the Mount Dean Stone funding request. And that was in addition to the $85,000 contributed through purchasing auction items, much to the excitement of Five Valleys' new Philanthropy Director, Whitney Schwab.

"New cornerstone: Dean Stone Mountain deal doubles Missoula open space," was the headline that accompanied reporter Rob Chaney's May 21, 2016, *Missoulian* story about the project. In Chaney's article, Kier mused about the opportunity and what it could portend.

"We don't have an answer about who will finally own this. It will be kind of lengthy and messy, because it will take a while to find the right fit. This is a potential model to rethink the way we do open space," Kier said.

The next step was getting the community excited about a broader vision for the mountain, as Five Valleys had done with Mount Jumbo, Mount Sentinel, and so many other acquisitions. To do that, Five Valleys had to get the public up onto the South Hills Spur, and do so by trail, avoiding direct access by motor vehicles.

It was the Barmeyer family who made that possible. Long time Five Valleys supporters and truly conservation-minded landowners, theirs was the second fateful call to come in during that two week span in 2014, when they contacted Five Valleys to explore the idea of protecting their family's land in Pattee Canyon.

The Barmeyer family property shares part of the north-south boundary of the South Hills Spur parcel. In conjunction with conservation easements placed on two distinct parcels of their land in 2016, access to the Spur was achieved. Provisions in the easement included the right to build a connecting trail from Pattee Canyon Road to the Spur. Subsequently the Barmeyers also gifted a portion of the protected land to the City of Missoula. At the same time, the city made Five Valleys whole by purchasing the Spur parcel with 2006 Missoula City-County open space bond funds.

One more giant step was complete. There may have been a champagne cork or two popped on the Spur one beautiful summer evening after the purchase closed. Hoyt and new Five Valleys attorney Alice Jones handled the Barmeyer easements and all subsequent land transactions on the expanding Mount Dean Stone project once the Spur had been acquired.

The skies over Mount Dean Stone darkened just a bit in late 2016, when Five Valleys founding board member, and longest-serving board member, passed away. Chuck Tribe was a quiet force who insisted on professionalism, honesty,

The grand opening celebration of the Barmeyer Trail on the South Hills Spur, June 2018. *–Photo by Vo Von Sehlen, Five Valleys Land Trust collections.*

and real conservation. In the early years when resources and staff were sparse and an actively involved board was essential, Chuck was there to lend a hand in any way. When a new opportunity beckoned, he would walk into the office wearing a big grin, clap his hands together, and, in words as close to profanity as he could get, exclaim, "Hot damn, that's just great."

Back on Dean Stone, work soon began on design and construction for a 3-mile-loop trail that would start at a trailhead adjacent to the Barmeyers' front gate, gently ascend and top out on the Spur, and wind back down to the trailhead completing the loop.

The saying "it takes a village" is the best description of trail building on Mount Dean Stone. Five Valleys, the City of Missoula, and the Montana Conservation Corps joined with Mountain Bike Missoula, which was simultaneously building trails on Marshall Mountain, to complete the beautiful Barmeyer Trail. In June of 2018, the Barmeyer Trail opened to the public. The trail became an immediate success with the pedestrian and biking public.

"I think people are thrilled to have access out their door on the south side of town, especially with the growth that's happening," Whitney Schwab told the *Missoulian* in a June 24, 2018, article about the opening of the Barmeyer Trail.

While the community response to the South Hills Spur was generally enthusiastic, some neighbors expressed concern about the changes this open space effort could bring to the neighborhood. Five Valleys worked to address these concerns in a variety of ways, including taking steps to prevent trespassing and illegal off-road vehicle use, and later conducted forest thinning to reduce the risk of wildfire and improve habitat. The South Hills Spur deal also limited trail construction near the closest homes to provide a buffer between public and private uses. The South Hills Spur and the ever- growing Mount Dean Stone project that followed emphasized a spirit of cooperation and compromise that will benefit Missoula community members for generations to come.

From the Spur, the next order of business was somehow getting a trail up to the top of Mount Dean Stone, or near enough for the visitor to feel as if they have been to the top.

The effort to get to the top would require vision and conviction on the part of the Board of Directors. As it ever had been, the Five Valleys Board was not only visionary, but engaged in the day-to-day workings of the organization. With the addition of a new cohort of community leaders, the board of the mid-2010s now included Mary Babson, David Banks, Lucy Beighle, Jim Brown, Ken Burd, Jim Cusker, Mary Lynn Eiseman, Juile Fogarty, Mike Foote, Julie Gardner, Denny Iverson, Kathy McAllister, Tom McDonald, John Rimel, Jeff Roth, Amber Sherrill, Pam Volkmann, and Rick Wishcamper.

With their support, new conservation easement projects were being developed and completed in and around public acquisitions work. From Lolo to Arlee to Seeley Lake and nearly every place in between, Five Valleys staff were engaged in working with private landowners on easements for agricultural lands and wildlife habitat. When the ink was barely dry, stewardship staff stepped in to ensure the continued protection of these precious places. Each of these projects came replete with rich history and important natural resource values, as well as with the stories that link the people with the land.

In Grass Valley, lifelong rancher Joe Boyer placed his fourth Five Valleys conservation easement on a portion of his historic family ranch on Roman Creek, bringing the total protected acres on the Boyer Ranch up to more than 1,200 acres. It was there, in 2016, that Joe spotted a pair of trumpeter swans and five cygnets among the cattails on the creek. Longtime board member and Five Valleys Audubon Society member Jim Brown confirmed that this was the first time trumpeters had been documented nesting in the greater Missoula or Bitterroot Valleys. One can be certain

Joe Boyer on his Roman Creek conservation easement property, 2012. *–Five Valleys Land Trust collections.*

the Salish once admired the giant white birds across the entire region, long before white settlers arrived. But the pair on the Boyer Ranch was proof of conservation and reintroduction success, which was greeted with much excitement.

An unexpected transition occurred in fall of 2017 when Grant Kier resigned as executive director in order to make a run for Montana's lone congressional seat. Five Valleys land protection staff had added sixty-nine new conservation easements to the land trust's portfolio during his tenure. Five Valleys now had a staff of ten and had protected over 83,700 acres across west-central Montana.

Kier's bold initiatives, the Confluence, Marshall Mountain, the Lincoln Community River Park, and, of course, Mount Dean Stone, combined with the ongoing conservation easement work, cemented Five Valleys' reputation as a respected community institution, while setting the stage for an even more exciting conservation future.

Amber Sherrill, a fifteen-year board member and then president of the Five Valleys Board, was asked to serve as interim executive director. Another longtime board member, Julie Gardner, was elected board president. The decision was based on plans for another open space bond request to go before the voters in November 2018. Five Valleys had again taken a lead role, and the board decided it would be too disruptive to launch a search for a new director during the bond campaign. With plenty of support and bond campaign experience available on staff, Sherrill and Gardner ably represented Five Valleys throughout the campaign, as the community once again overwhelmingly approved a $15 million open space bond. In a nod to perpetuity, city voters also approved a $500,000 annual stewardship mill levy to help care for existing conservation lands owned by the City.

Soon thereafter, Five Valleys began a nationwide search for a new executive director. Sherrill stayed on until it became apparent that the search would be prolonged, and former executive director Greg Tollefson stepped in for six months as the search continued. Sherrill would go on to be elected to the Missoula City Council, where she would continue to be a champion for conservation.

In the interim, Five Valleys staff did what they had always done by focusing on the work. Shortly after Kier's departure, project manager Vickie Edwards finalized the organization's fifth conservation easement in the Woodworth Meadows area south of Seeley Lake in partnership with the Rich and Cahoon families of Rich's Montana Guest Ranch, a homegrown outfitting and guiding business.

Edwards, who had joined the staff in 2014 after many years working for Montana FWP as a wildlife biologist, also finalized conservation easements with Oxbow Cattle Company at the mouth of Miller Creek, with conservationist Betty Thisted in the Ninemile, and a second easement with Anna Marie Hayes-Harrison in Potomac, among others, between 2017 and 2019.

In the Upper Clark Fork and Flint Creek Valleys, landowners were reaching out to Five Valleys with interest in conservation easements at a breakneck pace. Project manager Sarah Richey had recently completed a highly complicated series of conservation easements and servitudes with the Open Cross Ranch, protecting just shy of 5,000 acres in the heart of the Flint Creek Valley near Hall. A few months later, Richey would bring two more Flint Creek Valley projects to completion with the Buxbaum Ranch near Maxville and J T Ranches just across Highway 1 from Philipsburg.

This work in the Flint Creek Valley was the fruit of Five Valleys' Flint Creek Valley Initiative. Five Valleys and the Rock Creek Trust had worked around the edges of the Flint Creek Valley for decades protecting private properties along the Clark Fork River, Rock Creek, and Upper Willow Creek. Recognizing the Flint Creek Valley's vast grasslands, interlacing creeks, and rural character were still largely intact, Kier and staff had undertaken a study of the Philipsburg and Flint Creek Valley area. Funded by the LOR Foundation, the resulting report found the valley's rich natural resources and community's love of place and their agricultural heritage made it a prime place for Five Valleys to focus its efforts. With the completion of the Peterson Angus Ranch project and Sarah Richey's recent project accomplishments, the Flint Creek Valley Initiative was fully underway and continuing to grow.

Nearby, the Graveley family on the Little Blackfoot River near Garrison worked with Five Valleys, The Conservation Fund, the Montana Natural Resource Damage Claim Program, Montana FWP, and the Heart of the Rockies Initiative to complete a vision ten years in the making when they conserved 5,167 acres of their ranch. Using the proceeds from the conservation easement, the Graveleys then purchased and protected an adjoining 3,100 acres held by The Conservation Fund for that purpose. When the dust settled on the complicated transaction orchestrated by Sarah Richey, the Graveley Ranch became the largest conservation easement project Five Valleys had completed to date at 8,267 acres.

Shane and Sandy Graveley on their conservation easement property near Garrison. *–Five Valleys Land Trust collections.*

Closer to the Five Valleys headquarters in Missoula, Pelah Hoyt, when she was not busy with Mount Dean Stone, was completing a number of other exciting and important projects. On the far-west edge of Missoula's North Hills above Grant Creek, a choice 124-acre property with views of the entire Missoula Valley and the potential to connect to future trails on the Allied Waste conservation easement and beyond was put on the market. Once approached however, the conservation-minded landowners, J. Grant Lincoln and Gary D. Cooney, preferred that the land become public open space rather than privately developed. Working with the landowners, The Conservation Fund, attorneys at Boone Karlberg P.C., and with the guidance of board member Rick Wishcamper, Five Valleys moved quickly to purchase the land as an interim owner with the aim of transferring it to the City of Missoula. The Bluebird Preserve was transferred to the City of Missoula in the fall of 2019 with the support of open space bond funds. In addition to spectacular views of both Missoula and the Rattlesnake Wilderness, the property now provides a public trail and habitat for a variety of grassland species, including rare Missoula phlox, elk, and, of course, bluebirds.

More change was afoot when, in early 2019, Ryan Chapin, who had served as stewardship director and general jack-of-all-trades for Five Valleys for a decade, moved on to a new job with the Rocky Mountain Elk Foundation. He left the stewardship program in the very able hands of Jenny Tollefson.

In October of 2019, Jenny Zaso was installed as the executive director, only three months before the COVID pandemic upended life around the globe. Like most other businesses, Five Valleys locked the office doors and staff worked remotely from their homes as best as they could manage. Stewardship work had to take into account the variety of responses from landowners regarding face-to-face meetings on conservation easement properties. The tumultuous times also resulted in organizational changes. Jenny Zaso moved on and Whitney Schwab, the Five Valleys' philanthropy director, assumed the role of executive director.

"We've got a tremendous amount of work underway, particularly on Mount Dean Stone and in our greater service area like the Flint Creek Valley," Schwab told the *Missoula Current* in a June 3, 2020, article. "Five Valleys has a legacy of accomplishing important conservation, and we have a tremendous scope of work ahead. Our momentum is great, and so are our opportunities."

Schwab inherited a talented staff of twelve, which now included Forrest Boughner, operations manager; Vickie Edwards and Sarah Richey, conservation project managers; Pelah Hoyt as lands director; Alice Jones, staff attorney; Jenny Tollefson, stewardship director; Ryan Stutzman, conservation easement manager; Ramey Kodadek, annual campaign director; Lena Viall, development and communications coordinator; Patience Grant, office manager, and Katy White, events contractor. The organization had huge projects and initiatives underway, as well as a new landscape altered by the COVID pandemic. Schwab rose to the occasion admirably.

The Bluebird Preserve in the North Hills above Grant Creek. *–Photo by Brian Christianson, Five Valleys Land Trust collections.*

The 2019 Five Valleys staff and friends at Primm Meadow. From left: Vickie Edwards, Jenny Tollefson, Lena Viall, Pelah Hoyt, Sarah Richey, Greg Tollefson, Alina Niklison McCue, Alice Jones, Whitney Schwab, Katy White, Forrest Boughner, Ramey Kodadek, and Lalo Niklison. *–Five Valleys Land Trust collections.*

Meanwhile, the Mount Dean Stone project had continued to move slowly, farther and farther up the mountain. Pelah Hoyt had proceeded to work with landowners above the South Hills Spur to stitch a good trail route to the highest ridge.

By late 2019, with generous contributions from Five Valleys easement landowners Allen and Candace Fetscher, Bruce and Nancy Bugbee, and the family of late, longtime supporters Natalie and Jack Lyon, as well as direct or bargain sale purchases of the remaining parcels, the trail corridor had finally reached the ridge and continued around the summit, providing for a future trail loop. Members of the Line family, whose ranch abuts the trail corridor, were also key to finally reaching the top by working with Five Valleys to complete a land swap that added a key section to the trail and additional acres to the Line Ranch.

Much like the Confluence, Jumbo, or the Alberton Gorge, that sums up the series of very complicated transactions too easily. The Mount Dean Stone trail corridor required transactions with seven different landowners, including one national telecommunications company that first had to be convinced they even owned a portion of the mountain. Through sheer force, experience, and patience, Hoyt, with the capable assistance of Jones and the support of Schwab and the rest of the staff, made it possible.

Below, an alternate route to the Spur and beyond was also made possible with a bargain sale purchase from Dr. Mike Sousa. The narrow parcel off Spanish Peaks Drive allowed for a trailhead leading to a short trail segment that connected to the end of the Barmeyer Trail on the South Hills Spur.

In fulfilling Kier's prophetic 2016 *Missoulian* quote about being "a potential model to rethink the way we do open space," staff had gone about doing just that. The Mount Dean Stone project had evolved into a true community partnership comprised of over twenty organizations, agencies, and individuals, including Five Valleys, The Nature Conservancy, the City of Missoula, Missoula County, Run Wild Missoula, Mountain Bike Missoula, Summit Independent Living, Backcountry Hunters and Anglers, Hellgate Hunters and Anglers, Montana Trout Unlimited, onXmaps, REI Co-op, Big Sky Brewing Company, Providence St. Patrick's Hospital, Montana Conservation Corps, Montana Fish, Wildlife & Parks, Montana State Parks, MPG Ranch, Sapphire Physical Therapy, and Rocky Mountain Development Group Inc. Those partners had united to form the Mount Dean Stone Committee to help guide the project with the broadest community input possible and the following action statement:

> *Mount Dean Stone is a community effort to sustainably expand public use and stewardship in response to ongoing community needs on nearly 4,200 acres of proposed and newly created community open space bridging the urban-rural divide on Missoula's southside. Mount Dean Stone aims to serve as the future model of conservation to sustainably maintain public access for humans on the landscape.*
>
> *The goal of the Mount Dean Stone project is to solidify our community's connection to our landscape, improve forest health and reduce wildfire risk at the edge of town, safeguard the next generation's access to the lands we depend upon for our rich quality of life, and protect wildlife habitat.*

In addition to supporting trail planning and building efforts, the Mount Dean Stone Committee engaged itself in landscape-wide wildlife, habitat, fisheries, forestry, and road surveys in order to protect natural resources and decrease the threat of wildfire alongside increasing public use. Using this data, the committee developed recreation and natural resource management plans and potential trail routes for the Mount Dean Stone project area. They also worked on community outreach and events and even developed a logo that portrays the mountain as viewed from downtown Missoula. To accomplish this work, the Mount Dean Stone Committee met regularly in the Montana Natural History Center's new Ellen Knight Sense of Wonder classroom next door.

The Mount Dean Stone logo as created by the Mount Dean Stone Committee. – *Graphic design by Hailey Faust, Five Valleys Land Trust collections.*

On the south side of Mount Dean Stone, with a purchase agreement in place to eventually buy the adjacent 2,500-acre Nature Conservancy parcel, Five Valleys and its partners were able to build new trails and enhance old roadbed routes that, should the vision become reality, would connect to the trail corridor being secured on the north side. A trail was established at Inez Creek, with the trailhead just off Upper Miller Creek Road. Soon after, the Mount Dean Stone Committee partners and dozens of volunteers dug a new trail from the Inez Trail to an overlook that provides outstanding views up and down the Miller Creek drainage. The overlook, named Legacy Point, was so named in honor of The Nature Conservancy's Montana Legacy Project, which had acquired the parcel.

Upstream from Inez Creek, the committee worked to improve access at Little Park Creek. This access was an old fire and access road that wound up into the mountain, switchbacking up the rugged canyon. The committee enhanced the trailhead area, securing an access agreement with Montana Department of Natural Resources and Conservation, which owned the small parcel where the trailhead was located between Upper Miller Creek Road and The Nature Conservancy lands.

Across the road, the committee took a page from the Confluence story, and partnered with Summit Independent Living to build a 1/4-mile, universal access loop trail above Miller Creek. Five Valleys' continued work with Summit had revealed a severe lack of non-urban trails suitable for visitors who live with disabilities.

The new Miller Creek Universal Trail was installed during a particularly cold and windy National Public Lands Day in late September 2019. Though tents blew away and fingers froze, over seventy-five volunteers loaded on shuttle buses that took them to the project site 9 miles up Upper Miller Creek Road. There volunteers dug trail, installed a wheelchair accessible gate, and pulled a literal ton of knapweed before enjoying a well-deserved barbeque lunch.

Back on the northside of the Dean Stone, Mountain Bike Missoula was once again hired to scratch a trail through the newly created 350-acre corridor leading from the South Hills Spur to just below the summit. Staff nicknamed the trail "High, Wide, and Handsome" for the mountain it was on and the views it boasted. Despite the raging pandemic, volunteers came out in force–and in facemasks–to finish the 5-mile trail section.

Unable to hold a spring banquet out of concern for the pandemic, Five Valleys did everything imaginable to build community enthusiasm and support for the work before it. Schwab and Kodadek orchestrated private tour after private tour of Mount Dean Stone to talk about the project and its potential.

In November 2020, the Missoula City Council unanimously voted to acquire the corridor and the High, Wide, and Handsome Trail using $462,500 from the new 2018 open space bond, in addition to $462,500 from an anonymous estate gift. The funds were matched by over $1.5 million in real estate, trail, and project facilitation contributions from Five Valleys supporters. A few weeks later, the parcel, now officially dubbed the Mount Dean Stone Preserve, and the renamed Mount Dean Stone Preserve Trail, were transferred to the City of Missoula. The north side of the visionary project was complete.

Volunteers build the Miller Creek Universal Trail, September 2019. *–Photo by Geoff Sutton, Five Valleys Land Trust collections.*

The view of the Bitterroot Valley from the Mount Dean Stone Preserve. *–Five Valleys Land Trust collections.*

THIRTEEN

IN THE SHADOW OF THE MOUNTAINS THE WORK GOES ON

THE 2020 CENSUS NUMBERS FOR MISSOULA COUNTY came in at 122,000, a jump of another 10% in just a decade. The restaurant over Rattlesnake Creek had come back to life as a 4Bs Family Restaurant, reviving memories of the past when the first 4Bs opened on West Broadway, and later gave way to as many as four locations in town at the same time. They still boast about the tomato soup. The "Famous Meatloaf Dinner" was going for $11.50. The famous tomato soup is still famous, too.

Pelah Hoyt, holding the record for the longest continuous employment of any Five Valleys staff member, made a gracious exit in 2021. Her mark is on the landscape of Missoula and the entire Five Valleys working area. In addition to her conservation activities, Hoyt was the unofficial keeper of the institutional memory of the organization, having kept up with Five Valleys from her youth in Arlee and Missoula. Always mindful of the debt all Montanans owe to the Native peoples who lived on this land long before the tide of white settlers began arriving in the early 1800s, she worked diligently to improve Five Valleys' relationship with the Confederated Salish and Kootenai Tribes. Hoyt continued this work, moving on to manage the Confederated Salish and Kootenai Tribes–Montana Water Compact through the Montana Department of Natural Resources and Conservation.

One of the first tasks Schwab undertook as director was strategic planning. Looking to the future amid the uncertainties of the COVID pandemic, and the rapid boom in population and land prices that came with people migrating to Montana, was no easy feat for the board or staff. Western Montana's conservation needs had grown and matured. Healthy wildlife populations needed not only habitat,

The J T Ranches ranch in the upper Flint Creek Valley. *–Photo by Dave Gardner, Five Valleys Land Trust collections.*

but also the ability to move freely across the quickly fragmenting landscape. Open lands and trails were in high demand, as was the growing call to ensure they were truly accessible to all. Five Valleys had a role to play in helping the region and its landowners adapt and prepare for a changing climate. And, as Five Valleys' portfolio of conservation lands grew, the task of responsibly stewarding those lands into perpetuity underpinned it all. Schwab's staff and the board, now led by President Jeff Roth, took those needs and developed a roadmap for how to achieve them.

The working landscape remained a priority for conservation easement protection, encouraged and enhanced by partnerships with state and federal agencies. Funding secured through programs such as the USDA's Natural Resources Conservation Service's (NRCS) Agricultural Land Easement program and Regional Conservation Partnership Program (RCPP), funded through the federal Farm Bill, as well as the State of Montana's Natural Resource Damage Claim Program, enabled Five Valleys to work successfully with numerous ranch families to secure easement protection of important lands and assure continued viability of multi-generation ranching operations.

In 2021, Five Valleys was awarded a landmark NRCS RCPP grant of $3.7 million to further its work in the Flint Creek Valley. "It couldn't have come at a better time," according to conservation project manager Sarah Richey. Land values were escalating, as residential development increased as a result of the pandemic and

Kristin Vogel and her 1st grade class on B Hill. *–Photo by Lena Viall, Five Valleys Land Trust collections.*

other factors, and well-managed agricultural operations came under increasing development pressures. In this case, a lot of acronyms turned out to be a good sign and meant real conservation opportunities. It's important to know that the agricultural values of those lands do not stand alone when it comes to protection. Each easement also protects wildlife habitat, wetlands, scenic values, and often, but not always, recreational values, such as hiking, hunting, and fishing.

Throughout its working area, Five Valleys continued to reach out to landowners and communities to identify and address conservation opportunities, from agriculture to recreation to wildlife habitat and water quality, and just plain, invaluable scenic open spaces.

Overlooking the industrial town of Bonner, "B Hill," as it is known by the locals, fits into this category. In November 2021, Five Valleys completed the protection of this hardworking hill through a transaction with the previous landowner, The Nature Conservancy, and the new landowner, Bonner Property Development, which had come to own and revitalize the old Bonner lumber mill yard. The B Hill project was unique in that the conservation easement also included a perpetual public access easement held by Five Valleys. Now, in partnership with the current and future landowners, Five

Mount Dean Stone, as seen from McCauley Butte. *–Photo Mark Mesenko, Five Valleys Land Trust collections.*

Valleys will forever ensure that the Bonner community can use and enjoy B Hill.

Back on Mount Dean Stone, the Mount Dean Stone Preserve Trail had its grand opening in June of 2021. Looking ever forward, Five Valleys had been awarded a Montana FWP Recreational Trails Program grant to build the 4.6-mile House of Sky Trail that would unite trails across the whole network. Running along the ridge from below the summit of Mount Dean Stone to the West Fork of Deer Creek in Pattee Canyon, the route connected five trailheads: Barmeyer, Sousa, Inez Creek, Little Park Creek, and a newly renamed access point where the trail terminated, Skyline Ridge. Trail building commenced in the summer of 2021 and was completed in time for a grand opening on June 4, 2022, in honor of National Trails Day. While not wholly complete, the vision of a connected, protected Mount Dean Stone was a reality. The celebration

Ben Horan and Whitney Schwab on Mount Dean Stone. *–Photo by Martin Kidston,* Missoula Current.

also afforded plenty of opportunity to break a sweat and get in some good hard volunteer work. A great crowd showed up for both a little work and a good bit of fun on the mountain.

He may not have been able to walk the new trail, but John Talbot, another of the founding board members who gave long and distinguished service to the organization and passed away in December of 2021, was surely applauding its completion. John's quiet leadership over his seventeen years on the board was at the same time an inspiration and a source of reassurance that the organization's work was essential to the life and health of Missoula and western Montana. And John and Sue Talbot's generosity was often vital, especially in the early lean times, to keeping the Five Valleys ship afloat.

The new year, 2022, dawned with much excitement as it marked the fiftieth anniversary of Five Valleys Land Trust. It had been five decades since that group of twenty citizens formed the Five Valleys River Park Association out of love and

The twenty-sixth annual Banquet, held during Five Valleys' fiftieth anniversary year, was hosted at Washington-Grizzly Stadium on the University of Montana campus. The main event tent can be seen at center field. *–Photo by Dave Gardner, Five Valleys Land Trust collections.*

concern for the Clark Fork River. Luck would have it that the nightmare of the COVID pandemic was waning, and preparations were made to hold the annual banquet in-person once again. This would not be just any banquet, however. Staff were determined to go big or go home during such an auspicious year and held the annual event on the field of Washington-Grizzly Stadium on the UM campus. Invitations were sent out proclaiming that the community would join Five Valleys "on the 50-yard line to celebrate 50 years of conservation." Over 600 people did, selling out the limited number of tickets in mere days.

Throughout the year, in addition to moving projects forward, the staff moved mountains to mark and celebrate the occasion. At Rock Creek, the organization celebrated a full decade of ownership, restoration, and public access at the Confluence during the annual summer open house. An oral history project, led by Lena Viall, sought to capture the stories of founders, landowners, staff, and board members who had made the land trust's successes possible. A special fiftieth anniversary logo was created which adorned banners on streetlights along Higgins Avenue and Beartracks Bridge in downtown Missoula.

The fiftieth anniversary Five Valleys Land Trust logo. *–Five Valleys Land Trust collections.*

To meet the challenges and opportunities provided by the next half-century, Five Valleys launched the Montana Forever Campaign. The ambitious campaign was led by a special fundraising committee, headed by board secretary Julie Fogarty and Big Sky Brewing Company owner Bjorn Nabozney and with staff leadership from Philanthropy Director Ramey Kodadek. The campaign's goal was to raise $4.5 million to support the conservation work that was on the horizon and beyond. The campaign would conclude just sixteen months later, having raised a total of $4.523 million thanks to the generosity of over 230 donors, businesses, and organizations.

In October, over 400 community members came out for a fiftieth anniversary celebration in the pole barn of the Line Ranch on the slopes of Mount Dean Stone, complete with a live band, barbecue, and a dunk tank. Supporters young and old gathered to savor and celebrate a half century of the successful community endeavor.

Of course, it was back to work as usual come Monday morning.

Amid the celebrations, progress was also made toward completing the acquisition of The Nature Conservancy lands on Mount Dean Stone. Building off their half-decade of collaboration, the Mount Dean Stone Committee came together to develop a Mount Dean Stone Management Framework to guide Five Valleys or any other future owner of open lands on the mountain. Then, August of 2022 brought the great news that Five Valleys had been awarded a $600,000 grant from the competitive USFS Community Forest and Open Space Program. This grant, as well as a $100,000 grant from the Montana Fish and Wildlife Con-

Five Valleys' fiftieth anniversary celebration at the Line Ranch, October 2022. *–Photo by Anna Schreck, Five Valleys Land Trust collections.*

Melany Glossa, USFS Deputy Chief Executive for the Work Environment and Performance Office, and Tim Garcia, USFS Deputy Regional Forester for the Northern Region, walk on the House of Sky Trail, on Mount Dean Stone, June 2023. *–Photo by Lena Viall, Five Valleys Land Trust collections.*

servation Trust, would help provide key funds to purchase The Nature Conservancy lands above Miller Creek.

Over the next ten months, new Associate Director Ben Horan, previously the director of Mountain Bike Missoula, worked with partners and funders to steadily move the acquisition towards the finish line. In June of 2023, just as the beargrass began to bloom, Five Valleys acquired 2,470 acres between the ridgeline and Miller Creek and created the Mount Dean Stone Community Forest. A celebration was held at the new Skyline Ridge Trailhead to commemorate the occasion.

"We're at the dawn of a new era here," Schwab told reporter Joshua Murdock in the June 29, 2023, edition of the *Missoulian*. "We've worked diligently as a community to get up to this ridgeline."

Always a partner, The Nature Conservancy sold the parcel at a bargain sale price. This generosity, combined with Five Valleys' fundraising efforts, enabled the creation of a dedicated stewardship fund that would help Five Valleys, or any future owner, manage the valuable tracts of forest land for local community needs, including public recreational access, forest health and wildfire safety, economic benefits, and protection of vital wildlife habitat.

"Our commitment is to continue working with the community partners to find the best outcome for the landscape and the community," Horan told the *Missoulian*. "The Community Forest Program is the kind of funding tool that seems tailor-made for a community like Missoula. It has a strong emphasis in protecting community use on landscapes that are at risk of losing it."

With the creation of the Mount Dean Stone Community Forest, the larger Mount Dean Stone project that had begun as a private easement project with the Barmeyer family on the floor of Pattee Canyon had achieved its goal. Habitat had been protected and public access had been established across the entire Mount Dean Stone landscape, from the valley bottom to the summit and down again into the watershed on the opposite side of the mountain. The decade-long project had involved 17 unique land transactions totaling 3,058 acres, engaged dozens of stakeholders through the Mount Dean Stone Committee, mobilized hundreds of volunteers, and had ignited the enthusiasm of the broader community whose generosity made the project possible.

As the fifty-first year of Five Valleys Land Trust drew to a close, the organization had protected 100,381 acres of towering mountains, free-flowing streams, and productive agricultural lands. The land trust continues to restore and enhance the Rock Creek Confluence for the betterment of wildlife and the benefit of the community. The Lincoln Community River Park and Marshall Mountain have become open spaces ingrained in the fabric of the communities that love them. And across ten counties, stewardship staff ensure the perpetual protection of nearly 200 conservation easement properties.

As of this writing in 2024, the Five Valleys Board and staff, filled with the same passion for the wonder and beauty of this place that has been the heartbeat of Five Valleys from the very beginning, currently includes:

Board of Directors:
Denny Iverson, *Board President*
Allan Frankl, *Board Vice President*
Julie Fogarty, *Board Secretary*
Rachel McDonough, *Board Treasurer*
Jennifer Boyer, *Board Member*
Tyler Courville, *Board Member*
Elizabeth Fricke, *Board Member*
Mike Foote, *Board Member*
Addrien Marx, *Board Member*
Dan Pletscher, *Board Member*
Shaun Radley, *Board Member*
John Rimel, *Board Member*
Jeff Roth, *Board Member*
Stanley Senner, *Board Member*
Jessica Welborn, *Board Member*
Rick Wishcamper, *Board Member*

Staff:
Whitney Schwab, *Executive Director*
Ben Horan, *Associate Director*
Jenny Tollefson, *Stewardship Director*
Ramey Kodadek, *Philanthropy Director*
Sophia Barnes, *Development Coordinator*
Kit Fischer, *Senior Conservation Project Manager*
Julie Gilchirst, *Office and Events Administrator*
Derek Goble, *Conservation Project Manager*
Mari Houck, *Land Steward*
Minette Johnson, *Planned Giving Officer*
Ryan Stutzman, *Conservation Easement Manager*
Lena Viall, *Conservation and Communications Manager*
Boston Wakeham, *Operations Manager*

The work goes on.

The 2024 Five Valleys Board and staff. From left Allan Frankl, Dan Pletscher, Mike Foote, Jenny Tollefson, Ben Horan, Denny Iverson, Ramey Kodadek, Tyler Courville, Shaun Radley, Mari Houck, Minette Johnson, Derek Goble, Julie Fogarty, Sophie Barnes, Boston Wakeham, Julie Gilchrist, Ryan Stutzman, Addrien Marx, Kit Fischer, Lena Viall, Whitney Schwab, Jeff Roth, Martin Oakland. *–Photo by Anastasia Wilde, Five Valleys Land Trust collections.*

Elk and calf on western Montana open lands. *–Photo by Jason Savage Photography.*

PROTECTED PUBLIC LANDS

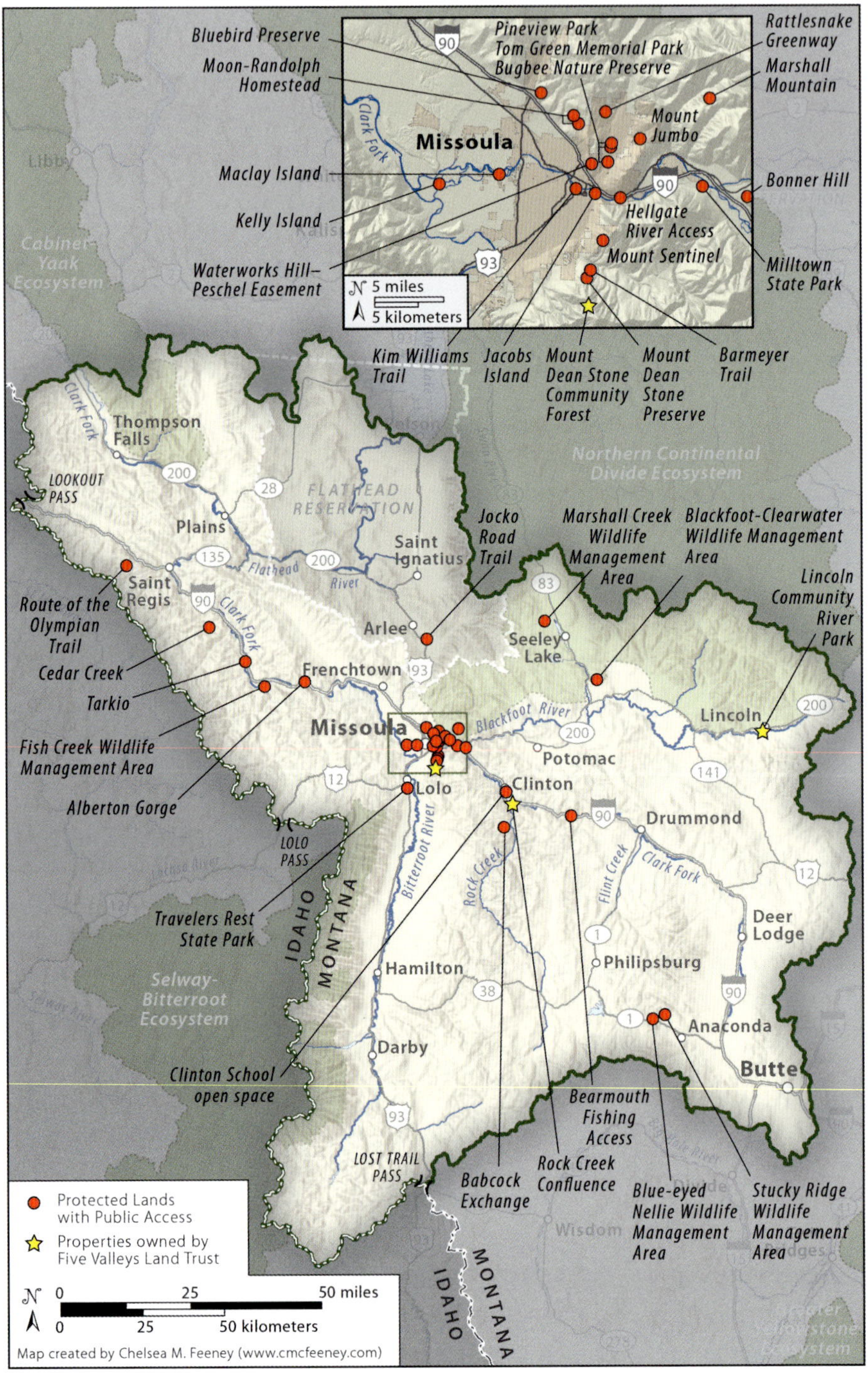

MISSOULA AREA PROTECTED LANDS

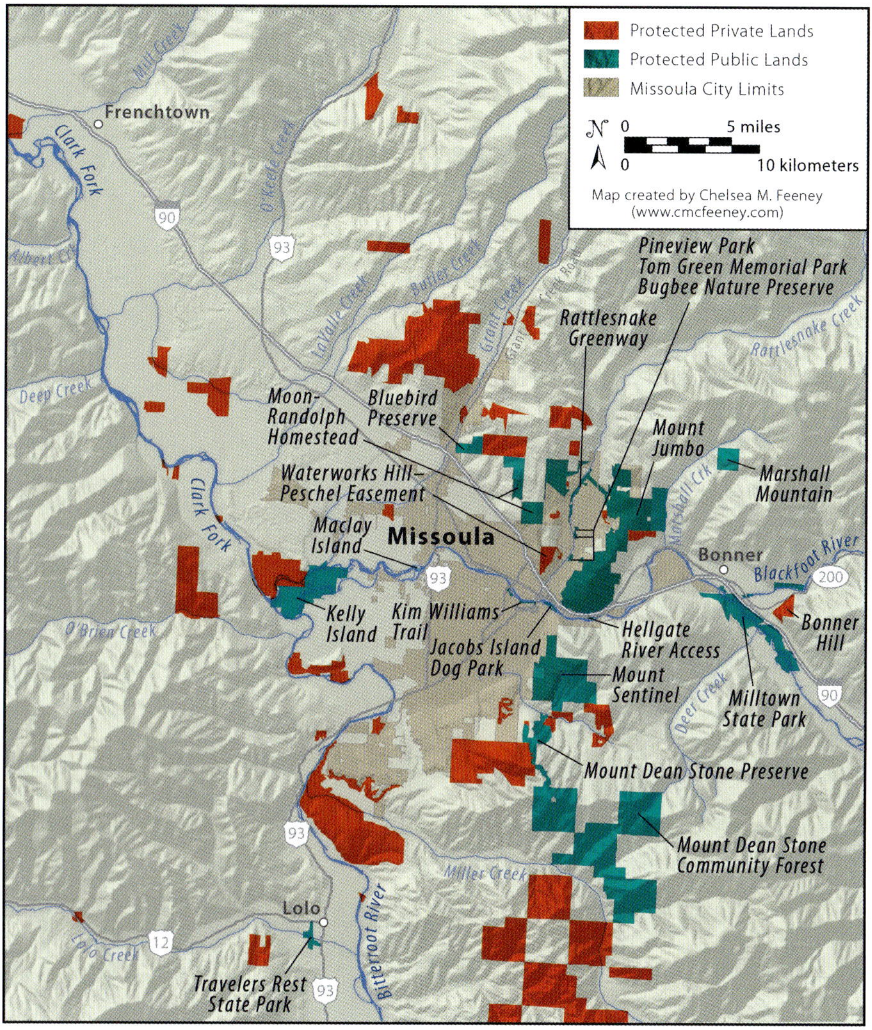

ALL PROTECTED LANDS

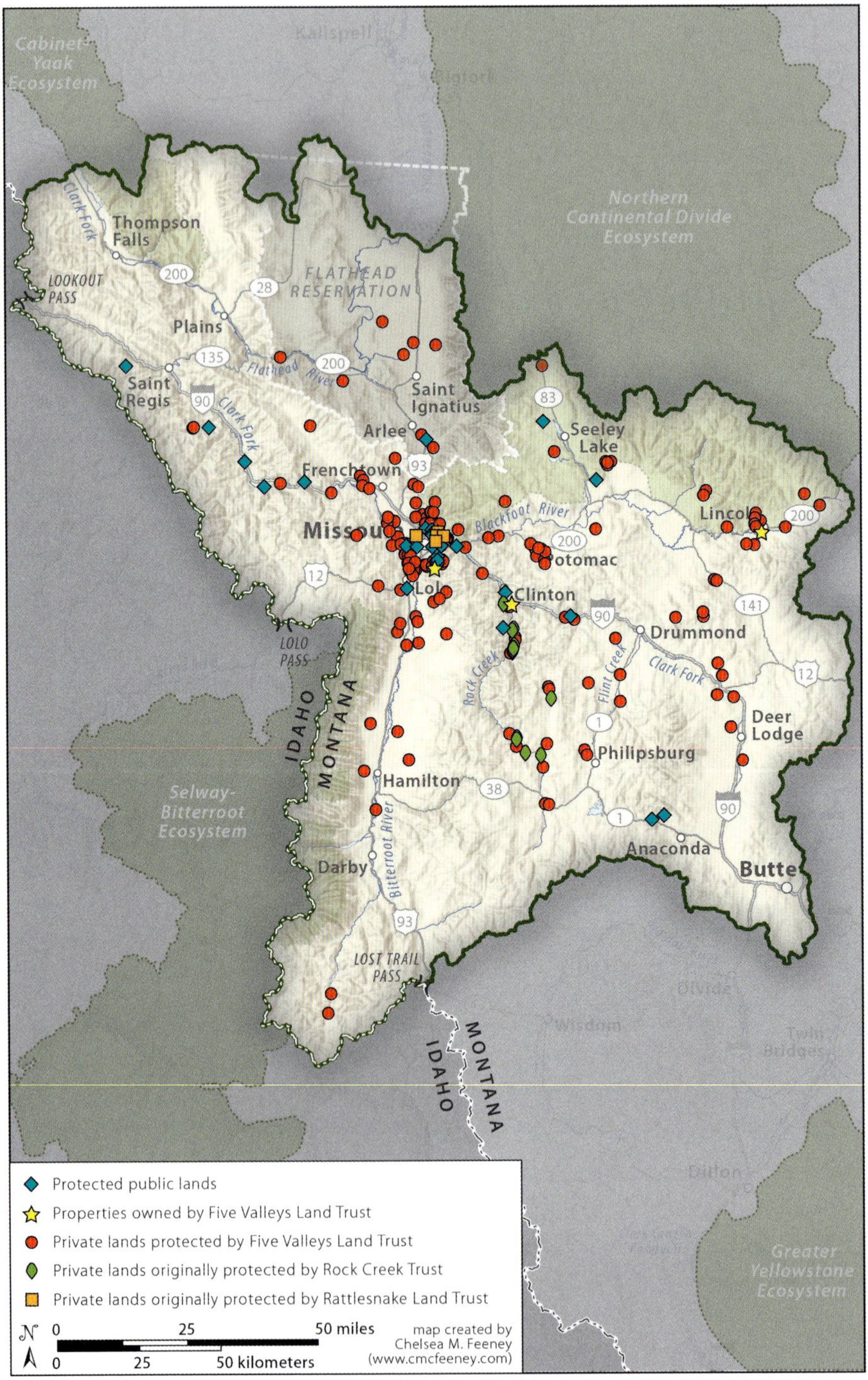

Bob Knight, Ellen Knight and Greg Tollefson. *–Photo courtesy of Greg Tollefson.*

EPILOGUE

SPIRIT OF THE PAST—VISIONS FOR THE FUTURE

MOST OF US HERE IN MONTANA, in any corner of the state, share a love of our home communities, our local landscapes, and Montana at large. Even folks who may be just visiting sense something special here. John Steinbeck, in his book *Travels with Charley: In Search of America,* put it this way: "I'm in love with Montana. For other states I have admiration, respect, recognition, even some affection. But with Montana it is love. And it's difficult to analyze love when you're in it."

Well, that sort of love of a place came home to roost in Missoula in the winter of 1972.

It was really such a simple idea in the beginning.

We live in a beautiful place, rife with natural wonder, but change is coming too fast. We need to protect what is wonderful, inspiring, and fundamental to living in such a blessed place as the Missoula Valley and the rest of the Five Great Valleys of western Montana. Let's make a plan and do that.

What was not so simple was creating an organization that would eventually become a trusted community institution and evolve and grow with the times, broadening its scope of work and aspiration, enduring through economic, social, and political upheavals, and facing and overcoming countless seemingly impossible challenges.

But that's what happened, starting with that fateful meeting in 1972, and continuing on for the next five decades.

It happened because the people who loved a place and shared a dream, time after time, stepped forward and said: "I want to help. I want to be a part of this. What do I need to do?"

It happened because the Missoula community rallied in support of the embryonic vision of an interconnecting system of parks and trails along the rivers and streams of the Missoula Valley. And as the community grew to encompass ten counties of western Montana, and their great rivers and sparkling streams, lofty mountains, grasslands, timberlands, and wetlands, rich soils and sparkling lakes, residents all across the Five Great Valleys joined in the effort.

When one revisits, or perhaps hears for the first time, the story of Five Valleys Land Trust, it is impossible not to see the recurring pattern of community members stepping into the breach, over and over again, to give of their time, their intellect, and their treasure in the service of a shared vision for the future of a place that has always seemed so very special to those fortunate enough to have lived here. There has been a certain magic to what has happened with the organization from the beginning. Always, the right people have been in the right place at the right time to face the next challenge and keep the fires of passion glowing.

From the beginning of the FVRPA, the organization has been graced with some of the finest leaders and unapologetic visionaries that any organization could hope to attract. Many have received brief mention in this story telling, but far more have slipped in under the radar, often just the way they would have liked it to be.

In the early years, before hiring a staff was even a consideration, and later, when a bare-bones staff was all the budget could handle, board members had to be on the ground, spreading the gospel of community conservation, sharing their knowledge, helping negotiate the deals, meeting with landowners and government officials, and cranking out the newsletters on an old mimeograph machine.

Of course they helped out in so many other ways, too, always born of shared passion for the place we are so fortunate to call home, and the job we have to protect it. Who can forget the lively bidding at the annual fundraiser for Elmer Frame's barrels of llama manure, Jim Valeo's biplane tours of the Five Great Valleys, Chuck Tribe's magnificently crafted canoes, Denny Iverson's beef, or Mae Nan Ellingson's lavish and wonderful dinners? And we can't forget Helen Bolle's pies.

A roster of the more than 100 individuals who have served on the Board of Directors of the organization since 1972 looks like an all-star team of the same community members who have charted the future of Missoula and western Montana in so many ways over the last half century. They have come from every conceivable walk of life, teachers, scientists, ranchers, farmers, homemakers, lawyers, physicians, bankers, resource managers, contractors, merchants, cooks, and even some bottle washers. What they all had, and continue to have, in common was keen intellect, shared sense of duty to the community and the natural world upon which our way of life is so dependent, and unlimited generosity of spirit.

Stories about individual board members and their contributions could fill volumes. And the same could be said for the many conservation professionals who have served on the Five Valleys staff since Amy Eaton Royer first took the helm in 1989. The hours are long, the work is difficult, sometimes extremely frustrating, and always much more complex than it would appear from the outside looking in. But when true passion for the work is the driving force, the rewards, when they come, can be almost beyond compare.

For the community members who have served on the board, the staff members, the landowners who have entrusted the future of their land with the organization, the countless partners from conservation groups, federal and state agencies, foundations and other funders, and the thousands of individual community members who have supported and worked with Five Valleys over the years, those rewards are often right out the front door.

All it requires is to lift the eyes for a moment and note the things about the beautiful landscape that have not changed in your memory, and note those things that one can now be assured will not change, whatever the future may bring. That is the reward. And the whole community should be proud of what it has accomplished.

And the work will continue, far into the future, always a "Gracious Civic Enterprise."

This story of our community and our landscape is dedicated to the memory of all who helped realize the vision of the founding mothers and fathers of the organization, but in particular, it is dedicated to the memories of Arnie Bolle, Betty duPont, Chuck Tribe, John Talbot, Jim Cusker, and Bob Knight, who never wavered from their dedication to conservation and community, and continue to inspire the work of Five Valleys, every day. And, the story is dedicated to Ellen Knight, who is still out there, quietly carrying the torch.

FIVE VALLEYS
LAND TRUST

Join Five Valleys Land Trust for our next half-century of serving western Montana. To learn more, get involved, and support our work, please visit our office in downtown Missoula, Montana, or online at fvlt.org.

Five Valleys Land Trust
120 Hickory Street, Suite B
Missoula, MT 59801
406.549.0755
fvlt.org

APPENDIX

Five Valleys River Park Association Directors (1972-1989):

Bender, Ronald
Bolle, Arnold
Bolle, Helen
Brabb, Geroge
Bradshaw, Stan
Browman, Audra
Bugbee, Bruce
Bugbee, Daphne
Bugbee, Nancy
Cardon, William "Bill"
Chinske, Cass
Closson, Jane
Collins, Thomas
Coutant, Gerald "Gerry"
Crawford, Bill
Crawford, Sue
Crow, Dave
Crowley, John
Denny, Evan
Field, Chris
Henry, Robert
Hubbell, Mark
Huggins, Jim
Jacobs, Randolph "Randy"
Jarvis, Gene
Jennings, Rudyard
Kelly, Dennis
Knight, Ellen
Knight, Robert "Bob"
Maclay, Helena
McCool, Steve
McDonald, Jim
McDowell, Joe
McKelvey, Robert
Meier, Joel
Neville, Robert
Nordbye, Louis
Ricer, Dean
Robbins, Jean
Spencer, Don
Talbot, Margot
Tobias, Carl
Toole, John
Turman, George
Turmell, Joseph
Williamson, Dennis

Five Valleys Land Trust Board of Directors 1989-2024

Babson, Mary, **2011-2013, 2016-2020**
Ballew, Will, **2008**
Banks, David, **2015-2023**
Beal, Kristine, **2001-2004**
Beighle, Lucy, **2009-2014**
Bender, Ronald, **1989-1996**
Benton, Sean, **2006-2014**
Bolle, Arnold, **1989-1994**
Boone, Ann, **2001-2007**
Boyer, Jennifer, **2022-Present**
Brehm, Laura, **2008-2010**
Brennan, Beth, **1993-1994**
Brown, Jim, **2008-2020**
Burchenal, Cooper, **2007-2008**
Burd, Ken, **2014-2021**
Burke, R.F. (Bob), **1989-1996**
Burner, Sandra "Sandy," **2006-2007**
Burnett, Gary, **2003-2004**
Clark, Ande, **2001**
Courville, Tyler, **2024-Present**
Corwin, John, **2009-2012**
Cusker, Jim, **2002-2022**
Demmons, Tom, **2000-2006**
Duerk, Amy, **2006-2008**
duPont, Betty, **1989-2005**
Eiseman, Charlie, **2006-2009**
Eiseman, Mary Lynn, **2011-2020**
Ellingson, Mae Nan, **1997-1999**
Fogarty, Julie, **2018-Present**
Fogel-Burchenal, Anne, **2009-2011**
Foote, Mike, **2017-Present**
Frame, Elmer, **1995-2002**
France, Tom, **1994-2003**

Frankl, Allan, **2020-Present**
Fricke, Elizabeth, **2022-Present**
Gardner, Julie, **2004-2019**
Harris, Dale, **1996-2000**
Henry, Robert, **1989-1991**
Hogan, Marcia, **1995-2002**
Hollenbeck, Scott, **1996-2004**
Holmes, Gary, **2000**
Iverson, Denny, **2013-2015, 2017-Present**
Jacobs, Randolph "Randy," **1972-1992**
Kenyon, Jim, **2008-2008**
Lane, Jocelyn, **2020-2020**
Lindbergh, Land, **1999-2001**
Luttschwager, Hal, **1989-1994**
Maclay, Helena, **1989**
Marx, Addrien, **2021-Present**
Masar, Susan, **1992-2005**
McAllister, Kathy, **2009-2020**
McDonald, Tom, **2015-2017**
McDonough, Rachel, **2021-2024**
Menson, John, **2004-2008**
Morrison, David, **2000-2001**
Niklison McCue, Alina, **2012**
O'Connell, Phil, **1994-2000**
Pitcher, Ciche, **2007-2008**
Pletscher, Dan, **2021-Present**
Precht, Bob, **1997-1998**
Radley, Shaun, **2021-Present**
Reineking, Kim, **1999**
Riber, Julia, **2004-2007**
Rimel, John, **2016-2024**
Roth, Jeff, **2010-2016, 2019-2024**
Roush, Katherine "Kathy," **1989-1995**
Royan, Jim, **2008-2010**
Scibek, John, **2004-2007**
Senner, Stanley, **2021-Present**
Sherrill, Amber, **2003-2017**
Sokoloski, Don, **2005-2015**
Sousa, Mike, **1999-2000**
Talbot, John, **1989-2006, 2008-2013**
Tawney, David, **1989-1991**
Tessman, Kristin, **2017-2020**
Tollefson, Greg, **2015-2016**
Tribe, Charles "Chuck," **1989-2016**
Tribe, Virginia "Ginny," **1989-1993**
Triepke, Rod, **2001-2008**
Valeo, Jim, **2004-2015**
Volkmann, Pam, **1996-2002, 2010-2021**
Welborn, Jessica, **2023-Present**
Whaley, Bob, **1993-2005**
Winslow, Nancy, **2006-2008**
Wishcamper, Rick, **2017-Present**
Wolfe, Gary, **2002-2006**
Wright, John B "Jack," **1995-1999**

Rock Creek Trust Advisory Council Members 1986-2009

Anderson, Al
Bach, Paul
Beck, Ron
Burnett, Gary
Clough, Richard
Compton, Art
Corwin, John
Darby, Dave
Englund, Karl
Erp, John
Eudaily, Gary
Fassbender, Larry
Fischer, Carol
Fischer, Hank
Flynn, Jim
Gillies, Lorraine
Hall, Tim
Hansen, Dave
Harris, Dale
Hogan, Marcia
Holmes, Gary
Holt, Ira
Kier, Grant
Knight, Robert "Bob"
Lane, Terry
Long, Mack
Marchion, Chris
Massey, Gant
McBride, John
Menson, John
Morrison, David
Munther, Greg
O'Connor, Roy

Poziwetz, Jim
Prill, Ray
Reiland, Eric
Reineking, Kim
Sanders, Tom
Schoonen, Tony
Stone-Manning, Tracy
Tollefson, Greg
Tribe, Charles "Chuck"
Wetzel, Wayne

Rock Creek Trust Staff 1986-1996

Dupree, Beverly; *Rock Creek Trust Assistant,* 1998-1999

Gilliam, Rob; *Rock Creek Trust Assistant,* 1997

Knight, Ellen; *Rock Creek Trust Director,* 1986-2000

Winninghoff, Amy; *Rock Creek Trust Assistant,* 1997

Five Valleys Executive Directors

Eaton Royer, Amy, 1989-1992

Kier, Grant, 2008-2017

Ninteman, Wendy, 1998-2007

Schwab, Whitney, 2020-Present

Sherrill, Amber, 2017-2018

Stone-Manning, Tracy, 1992-1994

Tollefson, Greg, 1994-1997; 2019

Zaso, Jenny, 2019-2020

Five Valleys Land Trust staff members

Bagg Lutz, Angie; *Administrative Assistant,* 2001-2002

Barnes, Sophia; *Development Coordinator,* 2023-Present

Beltran, Bray; *GIS Specialist,* 2013-2014

Biehl, Holly; *Development and Outreach Coordinator,* 2011-2014

Berkey, Jim; *Stewardship and Land Protection Coordinator,* 2000-2007

Botzet, Madison; *Membership and Volunteer Coordinator,* 2022-2023

Boughner, Forrest; *Operations Manager,* 2019-2020

Bowman, Jean; *Development Director,* 2002-2004

Bronk, Grant; *Land Steward,* 2002-2006

Chapin Ryan; *Land Protection Coordinator,* 2008-2010; *Stewardship Manager,* 2010-2012; *Stewardship Director,* 2013-2018

Clawson, Krista; *Office Manager,* 2003

Cogswell, Beth; *Director of Operations,* 2011-2013; *Associate Director,* 2014-2016

Davis, Juniper; *Conservation Project Manager,* 2008-2010; *Conservation Project Manager and Staff Attorney,* 2011

Dittloff, David; *Outreach & Grants,* 2003-2004

Drummond, Elizabeth; *Administrative Assistant,* 2005-2006; *Events Coordinator,* 2007-2008; *Banquet Coordinator and Administrative Assistant,* 2009-2010

Duvall, Ali; *Project Assistant,* 1999-2001; *Operations and Outreach,* 2001-2002

Edwards, Vickie; *Conservation Project Manager,* 2015-2020

Eggeman, Scott; *Conservation Project Manager,* 2014

Fagan, Chris; *Land Protection Specialist,* 2006-2007; *Conservation Project Manager,* 2008

Fischer, Kit; *Senior Conservation Project Manager,* 2024-Present

Gilchrist, Julie; *Office and Events Administrator,* 2024-Present

Grant, Patience; *Office Manager,* 2014-2020

Greenwell, Eric; *Conservation Project Manager,* 2021-2023

Goble, Derek; *Conservation Project Manager,* 2023-Present

Horan, Ben; *Associate Director,* 2021-Present

Houck, Mari; *Land Steward,* 2023-Present

Hoyt, Pelah; *Land Steward,* 2006-2007; *Conservation Project Manager,* 2008-2012; *Lands Director,* 2013-2021

Humes, Noreen; *Mount Jumbo Coordinator, 1995; Development Director,* 1996-1999

Johnson, Minette; *Planned Giving Officer,* 2023-Present

Jones, Alice; *Staff Attorney,* 2014-2021

Kodadek, Ramey; *Annual Campaign Director,* 2018-2020; *Philanthropy Director,* 2021-Present

Kogan, Lewis; *Conservation Project Manager,* 2010-2013

Marangelo, Glenn; *Development Director,* 2005-2015; *Planned Giving Director,* 2015-2016

Niklison McCue, Alina; *Land Protection Coordinator,* 2008-2009; *Stewardship Manager,* 2010; *Operations Director,* 2016-2019

Mueller, Caralee; *Office Manager,* 2004

Nelson, Meg; *Development Director,* 2001-2002

Oakland, Martin; *Conservation Project Manager,* 2022-2024

Olivier, Claire; *Office Manager and Event Coordinator,* 2005-2006

Pederson, Ana; *Office Manager,* 2011-2012

Pitman, Maggie; *Conservation Director,* 2012

Printz, Meredith; *Office Manager,* 2007; *Office Manager and Outreach Coordinator,* 2008-2010

Quinn, Daniel; *GIS Specialist,* 2015

Richey, Sarah; *Conservation Project Manager,* 2012-2022

Schwab, Whitney; *Philanthropy Director,* 2015-2020

Shepard Seaton, Jillian; *Office Manager,* 2012-2013

Sihler, Paul; *Heart of the Rockies Coordinator,* 2003-2007

Smith, Minie; *Stewardship Director,* 1994-1997

Stutzman, Ryan; *Conservation Easement Manager,* 2020-Present

Tollefson, Greg; *Rock Creek and Special Projects Consultant,* 2003-2008; *Conservation Director,* 2009-2011; *Regional Director,* 2017

Tollefson, Jenny; *Stewardship Coordinator,* 2011-2012; *Land Steward,* 2013; *Stewardship Manager,* 2014-2019; *Stewardship Director,* 2020-Present

Triepke, Lisa; *Development Director,* 2000

Viall, Lena; *Development and Communications Coordinator,* 2015-2021; *Conservation and Communications Manager,* 2022-Present

Wakeham, Boston; *Operations Manager,* 2021-Present

White, Katy; *Office Manager,* 2021; *Development Coordinator,* 2022-2023

Conservation Easement Landowners

The work of Five Valleys would simply not be possible without the contributions, vision, and generosity of the private landowners who protected their properties with Five Valleys conservation easements. Out of respect for the privacy of these landowners, this book does not contain a list of all Five Valleys' conservation easement projects to date. Five Valleys extends our heartfelt—and perpetual—thanks to all of the nearly 200 easement grantors who have helped conserve western Montana's open lands.

INDEX

C

G

H

L

P

Q

R

T

U